FISHING BOATS OF WHITBY AND DISTRICT

by
Gloria Wilson

HUTTON PRESS
1998

Published by

The Hutton Press Ltd.,
130 Canada Drive,
Cherry Burton, Beverley
East Yorkshire HU17 7SB

Printed by
Burstwick Print & Publicity Services
13a Anlaby Road, Hull. HU1 2PJ

ISBN 1 872167 99 3

CONTENTS

For reasons of printing, the colour photos which fall in chapter 3 are in an arbitrary position.
The publisher apologises to the reader for the way they interupt the text.

PREFACE

This book sets out to illustrate some of the fishing boats which have been built and owned in the North Yorkshire port of Whitby and the adjacent coastal communities.

The topic is so huge that it has been necessary to make a selection from the hundreds of craft which would have been worthy of mention.

Although some of the early history of Yorkshire boats is touched upon, the author has drawn on her own experience and original fieldwork and so the book concentrates largely on the modern era from somewhere around the 1950s to the late 1990s with perhaps greater emphasis on some ports and localities than on others.

Rather than attempting a single chronological narrative the author has chosen to describe the different boat types separately but the earlier chapters look at the English square sterned cobles which are associated with the shelving beaches and tidal harbours and creeks of north-east England and are among the few traditional British inshore working boats to survive into the twentieth century.

Nevertheless, a variety of perhaps less widely known craft have been built to meet wide local circumstances and fishing requirements in various localities, so double-enders, mini keelboats and scrobs are described.

On the other hand, vessels constructed elsewhere, such as Scottish motor fifies and seiner trawlers have also proved suitable for particular tasks in the Yorkshire fleets and a selection of these are included.

Nothing much is mentioned of Whitby's wonderful history as a builder of wooden merchant ships and whaling vessels nor does the book deal with the great explorers, navigators, master mariners and whaling captains produced by the area.

These are vast topics covered by and still being researched by other writers and historians.

So the purpose of the book is to celebrate the attractive fishing vessels which have added greatly to the character and liveliness of Whitby and other seaboard towns and villages and to pay a tribute to the people who have built and handled them.

The region itself is one of remarkable contrasts. Some of the fishing communities exist within large industrial areas such as Redcar near the huge steelworking and petrochemical plants of Teesside, but between Saltburn and Scarborough the most complete sequence of Jurassic rocks in Britain offers spectacular scenery with great cliffs and headlands and deep ravines and bays and inlets.

Perilous shelving rocks called scars cause heavy breakers and surf sometimes well out to sea.

The charming and highly individual port of Whitby lies at the mouth of the river Esk which flows into the North Sea between high cliffs.

The North Sea is amongst the richest fishing grounds of all continental shelves. Herring, white fish such as cod, haddock and whiting, and also lobsters, brown crabs and migratory salmon have been fished extensively.

The author trusts that the book will help to further the growing enthusiasm for classic boats both as a subject for scholarly study and for considerable enjoyment and admiration.

ACKNOWLEDGEMENTS

I am grateful to the numerous friends and acquaintances who gave me the information which is used in this book.

It is impossible to name them individually as there are so many of them.

My special gratitude must go to the boatbuilders and fishermen who gave me such a great deal of their time and answered my queries so readily.

Thanks are also extended to the members of other branches of the fishing industry who were helpful and informative, and to those who responded to my letters.

Some fishermen and others who shared their knowledge with me in the earlier days are sadly no longer with us. They too were a wonderful source of information.

Gloria Wilsons
1998

AUTHOR'S NOTE

It is customary during the late 1990s to use metric measurements and weights but British equivalents are used in much of the book to avoid filling the text with a rash of brackets and decimal points.

All but the new boats were built to British dimensions and scantlings, and other information in the book dates back to pre-metric days.

A few principal equivalents are given here..

BRITISH		METRIC
1 inch	-	25.400 millimetres.
1 foot (12in)	-	304.800 mm.
1 yard (3ft)	-	914.40 mm
1 fathom (6ft)	-	1.829 metres
1 gallon	-	4.546 litres
1 pound	-	453.60 grams.
1 stone (14 lbs)	-	6.350 kilograms
1 hundredweight (cwt)	-	50.80 kilos
1 ton (20 cwt)	-	1.0160 tonnes

G.WILSON.

ENDURANCE WY89
was a particularly buxom English square sterned coble built by Gordon Clarkson in Whitby for the Staithes fleet in 1973.

6

1. YORKSHIRE LUGGERS, YAWLS AND COBLES

Storm battered

Situated on the rugged North Yorkshire coast some ten miles to the north west of Whitby the storm battered village of Staithes is built on the sides of a deep ravine where a small tidal river runs into the sea between two immense cliffs.

Tightly grouped houses are set all anyhow around yards and slopes and alleyways and byways and there are very many steps.

All manner of things are influenced by the sea and fishing. Some houses are named after boats, for instance Star of Hope Cottage, Confidence Cottage, Unity House, Blue Jacket House, Venus Cottage and Wavelet.

Some things are quirky. The warning to KEE POUT is painted on the door of a fisherman's shed.

In an artist's house a fireplace has tiles on which are painted the names of boats; SILVER LINE, LEADING STAR, STAR OF BETHLEHEM, NIL DESPERANDUM, MIZPAH, TOILER OF THE SEA and GOLDEN CROWN.

Highly sought-after models of local fishing cobles are displayed in the windows of cottages.

A wave hits the Cod and Lobster pub in the storm battered village of Staithes. Part of the building was washed away in the great North Sea storm in January 1953.
(Photo: author's collection)

Fishing paraphernalia and parts of boats were even used as house building materials. Masts and spars support roofs and ceilings, and in 1998 in a house being renovated the staves of fish barrels were found covering a hole under the rafters.

During bad weather the seas blast against the houses and storm up the slipways and along the cobbled high street, and the air is filled with spume.

On the bridge and alongside the small river, known locally as a beck, huddled groups of people watch anxiously the plunging boats and hope that none will break their mooring ropes.

Staithes is notable for several reasons. Future circumnavigator and explorer Captain James Cook RN was employed for about eighteen months in the village in 1745-6 before moving to Whitby.

Artists have always been fascinated by the locality, and the Staithes Group, based in the area around the turn of the nineteenth and twentieth centuries, typified the best in British Impressionist painting.

Some twenty five to thirty artists painted out of doors in all weathers, finding their inspiration largely in the dramatic scenery and the work of the fisherfolk and their vessels. Later the painter Lilian Colbourn produced highly individual and powerful pictures of fisherpeople and rough seas and the omnipresent seagulls.

Today the story of Staithes and of Captain Cook and his ships is wonderfully displayed in the Captain Cook and Staithes Heritage Centre, housed in the former Primitive Methodist chapel.

Significance

Early in the nineteenth century Staithes was the most important fishing port on the English east coast north of the Wash. Fishing assumed more significance in the Yorkshire coastal villages because the bigger ports of Whitby, Scarborough and Bridlington had developed vigorous maritime interests largely based upon building, owning and serving merchant ships although Scarborough had a fishing industry of some consequence, and Whitby's involvement with the Greenland whale fishery began in the mid eighteenth century and lasted with several breaks until the 1830s.

During the forty years spanning the turn of the eighteenth and nineteenth centuries Staithes owned as many as seventeen sturdy Yorkshire luggers equipped for line and herring drift net fishing and known as 'five man boats' because five shareholders were involved in their ownership.

In February or March these boats began line fishing primarily for cod, ling, haddock and turbot close to the Dogger Bank, an extensive shallow shoal lying some sixty miles off the north-east coast of England.

Fishing was done from two cobles which the bigger boat had carried to sea on her deck.

High quality 'salt fish', prepared by a complex dry curing process, was a Staithes speciality and in huge demand for export to Catholic countries.

Later in the year the five-man boats took part in the East Anglian herring fishery and were then laid up for the winter. Fishing may not have been their sole occupation. Smuggling of dutiable goods, including spirits, lace, tea, tobacco and silk, was rife in Staithes prior to 1820 or thereabouts, and customs officers kept an eye on these luggers.

Their rig made them speedy and able to outrun the revenue vessels. At least one Staithes five-man boat had a false bulkhead behind which contraband could be hidden.

Three masted

A splendid model in the Science Museum in London represents a Yorkshire lugger or five-man boat 61ft long between perpendiculars with a 19ft 6in beam.

She is fully decked, three masted and clinker planked, with bluff bow, curved stem, straight keel, fine run, round bilges, slightly hollow floors, short bilge keels and lute-type stern. The model carries large fairly low peaked dipping lug sails on main and foremast and a smaller topsail on the mainmast, though topmasts on fore and mizzen masts show they too could have carried topsails.

The standing lug mizzen is more sharply peaked.

The quadrilateral lug sails, with the yards slung in a fore-aft position, and only a narrow area of canvas forward of the masts, gave the boats good speed and weatherly qualities.

A capstan for hauling drift nets stands abaft the mainmast.

Some nineteenth century drawings which I have seen in a private collection suggests the Yorkshire luggers were beamy and full in the head for carrying capacity, and carried a bowsprit on which a jib sail could be set.

This model of a Yorkshire lugger or five-man boat is in the Science Museum in London.

A drawing by the nineteenth century artist George Weatherill, born near Staithes, shows a five-man boat with a wide lute stern.

Said to be superb seaboats these luggers could lie in heavy weather without running for shelter. Waves broke dangerously at the Dogger Bank.

About forty five-man boats were owned along the Yorkshire coast between Redcar and Bridlington in 1825. Staithes owned the most at seventeen.

Fish prices were high in the prosperous time after the Napoleonic Wars. Some twenty five-man boats, many for Staithes and the majority from boatbuilder John Skelton of Scarborough were built during the five years ending 1820.

Yawls

In general along the Yorkshire coast these large luggers were superseded by two-masted fully decked 'yawls' some 45 to 60ft long although Staithes favoured the five-man boats well into mid century.

The name 'yawl' referred to the boat type rather than her rig. Seakeeping qualities were still paramount and yawls could weather all but the harshest conditions.

Yawls were generally of leaner hull form than the five-man boats, with lute stern, fine run and fairly steep slightly hollow floors. They were high at the shoulder to meet the seas and had a somewhat deeper less rounded forefoot.

The lute stern, in which the run of the upper strakes extended abaft the transom gave protection in surf should the yawl be beached.

A typical yawl initially carried dipping lug mainsail, standing lug mizzen sheeted to a long outrigger and a jib on a bowsprit. The mizzen mast was forward of the rudder head.

Yawls were normally clinker built with joggled frames and floors, but bulwarks were carvel planked.

A gate in the bulwarks facilitated launch and retrieval of the one, or sometimes maybe two, cobles needed for line fishing. During herring drifting the warps were hauled by a capstan whose bars were usually turned by four men.

This was gruelling work and wooden treads nailed to the deck helped the men keep their footing.

Staithes acquired about a dozen new yawls during 1855-59 and more in the 1860s.

Clinker planked yawls built in Whitby for Staithes included the 59ft long and 17.3ft beam BLUE JACKET in 1857 for Joseph Verrill, and the similar sized VENUS for Daniel Cole in 1859 and the slightly larger 60.5ft by 17.4ft GOOD INTENT for Thomas Cole in 1863.

By this time the village owned some seventeen, two masted lug rigged yawls constructed mainly in Whitby and Scarborough.

Yawl ownership was divided into sixty-four shares. Joseph Verrill was main shareholder in BLUE JACKET, owning thirty-two shares for example.

More than a hundred yawls were owned on the Yorkshire coast in the 1860s the majority at Scarborough and Filey.

Sometime around this time the majority changed to a handier ketch rig with gaff mainsail, gaff and boom mizzen and one or two jibs. Topsails could be set above mizzen and mainsail, and the mainsail was sheeted to an iron 'horse' or bar spanning the deck forward of the mizzen mast.

The ketch rig afforded better manoeuvrability when some yawls tried trawling for white fish, but was later adopted by the non-trawling ports such as Staithes as fewer crewmen need be carried.

WILLIAM ASH WY1 was a typical Staithes clinker planked Yawl, built in Whitby in 1867. Note the coble on her deck.

Conflict

From the 1840s there were great changes in fishing activities and the outlets for catches.

The rapid expansion of railways meant that fish could be transported to inland destinations in Britain and made available for mass consumption in the growing industrial areas.

A vigorous Yorkshire herring fishery developed which by the late 1850s was amongst the most profitable in Great Britain with the season lasting nearly five months.

By 1860 a largescale trawl fishery for white fish was well established particularly from Hull and Scarborough though smaller ports including Staithes deplored the method.

Line fishermen held trawlers responsible for depleting fish stocks, killing spawn and undercutting the prices for fish.

Staithes fisherman James Fell, a witness to the Royal Commission on Sea Fisheries*, said in 1863 that trawled fish was 'not fit for human food..... it is all knocked to pieces and the gall bladders are all burst'. He said the Staithes yawls now fished 'further north' rather than near the Dogger where catches were virtually nil and lines would be towed away by trawlers.

'I would abolish them altogether and compel them to go a-fishing with long-line' he added.

At Staithes the line catches were said to be a quarter what they were ten to fifteen years earlier though prices were higher. Herring fishing was also threatened. Trawlers were claimed to kill herring spawn and cut the drift nets, and French herring fishermen with stronger boats and nets forced the Staithes drifters off the grounds and also worked on Saturday and Sunday which the deeply religious and chapel-going Staithes men did not.

The fisherfolk held rituals to ward off risks and perils. At Staithes a pigeon's heart stuck full of pins was burnt over a charcoal fire to bring better fortunes to an unlucky vessel.

Herring fishing by Yorkshire yawls dwindled generally in the 1880s partly because of their shape and build and rig. Their hull form, designed for seakeeping on the exposed lining grounds, and also their clinker planks and ketch rig made them slower than the visiting carvel-built Scottish herring luggers which could reach port sooner and catch an early market.

Line catches declined further and before World War 1 the last of the Staithes yawls worked lines in early summer and were laid up in Whitby for the remainder of the year.

*Report of the Commissioners appointed to inquire into the Sea Fisheries of the United Kingdom.
Vol 1, Report and Appendix.
Eyre and Spottiswoode for HMSO 1866.

Some activity

For much of the nineteenth century Staithes owned some seventy to a hundred cobles many for fishing nearer home with longlines and herring driftnets. In the early 1860s for instance some forty cobles worked longlines from November until March six to ten miles offshore on hard rocky ground.

But the coblemen's fortunes also collapsed in late century. Fishermen said that steam trawlers carried away lines and destroyed fish stocks. Things were made worse by a shortage of mussel bait and low fish prices.

Many Staithes men left fishing and found employment in the local ironstone mines.

Some activity continued.

Fisherman Matt Verrill told me in the 1970s that a dozen cobles were still fishing from Staithes when he first went to sea full time in the coble STAR OF HOPE WY174 in 1928. During the 1920s several cobles worked herring drift nets in addition to longlines and also crab and lobster pots.

Measuring 29ft 9in long with 7ft 9in beam STAR OF HOPE, built in Staithes by J T Cole in 1928 had a lug sail and a 9 horsepower Thornycroft petrol engine and fished until the early 1950s.

One former Staithes coble, SILVER LINE WY184, constructed in Filey in 1928 and later sold away from Staithes, was only broken up in Whitby in the 1990s where for a few years she had lain perishing obliquely alongside the river Esk.

In her day much admired for her pretty lines she was later vulgarised by the addition of fibreglass sheathing and a monstrosity of a wheelhouse.

Star of Hope WY 174 was one of the last cobles to be built in Staithes. She was smashed up in the great storm of 1953. (Photo: author's collection).

THE ENGLISH SQUARE STERNED COBLE

Cobles, more correctly known as 'English square sterned cobles' are still in use in the late 1990s though in drastically reduced numbers.

As a type, the coble is one of the few traditional British working craft to survive into the close of the twentieth century.

She is one of the most curious of British beachboats.

Her complex hull form enables her to cope with rigorous circumstances on shore and at sea along the inhospitable English coast between the rivers Tweed and Humber.

In addition to being a splendid seaboat she is ideal for launch and recovery stern to shore through heavy breaking surf and can also negotiate rollers and shallow breaking seas when entering or leaving unsheltered tidal harbours and creeks.

Curious and complex

Her forward and after parts differ in shape remarkably.

She has pronounced forward sheer with high, slightly curved forward raking stem and uncommonly deep rounded forefoot. Her entry is fine with lean hollow lines below the waterline and considerable flare and shoulder above.

Forming a continuation of the forefoot the part keel ends just abaft amidships.

Whitby built cobles in Staithes in 1978. In the background, left to right, are ENDURANCE, EMBRACE G and PILOT ME B. In the foreground are ALL MY SONS (left) and REPUS. Note; by this time ENDURANCE had a deck forward, which she did not have at the time of her building.

Left: EMBRACE WY 207 was built in Whitby for Staithes in the 1960s. Note her deep rounded forefoot, stout frames and broad strakes, and the long rudder and tiller all of which are typical coble features.

Below: The half-decked Staithes cobles CORONATION QUEEN WY 75 (left) and GOLDEN CROWN WY 78 were built in 1953 at Amble and Whitby respectively. Note their square sterns, tumblehome and broad strakes.

JANE MARIE WY 337 was built in 1982 at Sandsend for Redcar. Typical coble features include her braod strakes, raked square stern and the two drafts.

The entry is sufficiently fine to cut through the waves, whilst the flare and shoulder give lift in heavy seas and buoyancy when heeling.

The deep forefoot, lean entry and hollow underwater lines grip the seas for windward sailing.

When the coble is putting to sea or making a landing the full flare and shoulders lift her head so that she is not overwhelmed by the waves, and together with the high bow they prevent water breaking inboard.

At the water's edge the deep forefoot, sharp entry and hollow underwater lines help keep her head to sea and the forefoot digs into the sand and steadies the coble during retrieval.

The section of greatest beam generally occurs abaft amidships, and afterwards from here the coble has a shallow afterbody with flat floors and hard bilges.

Two side keels, or drafts, extend from just forward of amidships to the stern.

They facilitate launching and beaching, prevent her after end from digging into the sand, and hold her upright when ashore and can withstand a good bashing on the beach.

Strakes are uncommonly broad, and for much of its length the sheerstrake has a generous tumblehome which increases the degree to which the coble can heel before water falls inboard.

The sheerline curves up sharply aft and the horseshoe-shaped square stern is usually half the maximum beam and half the height of the stem and rakes aft at some 45 degrees.

All these characteristics enable the coble to be beached, rowed and sailed and later to adapt readily to motor power and also made her an excellent seaboat.

Sailing coble rig was simple, without standing rigging, though details varied.

Normal rig was a single large dipping lugsail having several rows of reefpoints. It was hoisted by a heavy rope halyard which was rove through a sheave in the masthead and secured to a traveller from which the yard was slung.

Survive a gale

Cobles could be dangerous in a big following sea or when running before the wind because the forefoot could gripe and cause her to broach and capsize.

But most cobles could sail unusually close to the wind and in the hands of experienced men they could sail long distances and survive a gale.

The dipping lug sail was one of the most strong and efficient and weatherly sails ever developed but it needed to be lowered and reset to the lee of the mast whenever the coble went about.

The lugsail could be lowered quickly in a squall. A bight in the halyard was given a turn around the sailing pin which pointed downwards from the outside gunwhale. The fall was jammed between the gunwhale and standing part of the rope so a quick pull would allow the sail to come down rapidly.

The mainsheet was not made fast but was taken around the inwire abaft the after thwart and held by the helmsman.

Set up on the weather bow the tack was held by a hook on the gunwhale or on a tack rope secured athwartships. A bowline kept the luff taught and helped the coble to point well up into the wind.

The mast could be raked further aft in poor weather or lowered when fishing.

Big cobles sometimes set a jib on a bowsprit and also carried a lug mizzen.

An uncommonly long rudder descended a good way under the hull and also functioned as a deep keel to grip the water and reduce leeways drift.

It could be lifted inboard quickly and easily before the coble came ashore and would move upwards if she grounded accidentally. The long tiller was shaped to slope into the coble and be within quick and easy reach of the helmsman.

Coble oars had an iron ring at one side of the loom which fitted over a thole pin in the sheer and were thereby captive and not lost should the oarsman let go.

Ballast, usually sandbags or stones, was carried by the sailing cobles.

Particularly in the nineteenth century, cobles came in all lengths from some 10ft to 40ft and even larger.

A length-beam ratio of 4:1 was usual for a medium sized sailing coble. TOILER OF THE SEA, built at Whitby in 1895 for Staithes measured 33.9ft with 7.9ft beam and carried lug and jib sails.

Cobles have been among the most numerous and widely distributed types of inshore boat and have worked from nearon thirty beaches and harbours and creeks along the north-east coast and perhaps reached their greatest number in the late nineteenth century.

Left: A small Whitby coble with her dipping lug sail.

Cobles in the Dock End in Whitby in the 1970s. They vary in line and detail but share many common features.

Uncertain

Historians are uncertain of the coble's origin.

There is a suggestion of Celtic skinboats, seen for instance in the flush stemhead and the way in which the gunwhale projects beyond the stern.

Yet much of her build indicates Dutch or Norse ancestry and the terms used for her components derive from various languages. The Oxford English Dictionary quotes use of the word coble in various spelling as early as c950 AD but no known writings prior to the nineteenth century describe the boat in any great detail. By the 1940s most cobles had a petrol motor, positioned forward of amidships to keep the shaft angle low and retain the boat's shallowness aft.

The propeller was housed between the drafts to shield it from damage ashore.

WHITBY COBLES; A STYLE OF THEIR OWN

During the forty-five years following World War 2 Whitby and district has had more coble builders than anywhere else.

In the late eighteenth century the port was a principal producer of merchant ships and in 1792-93 became second largest builder in England for the tonnage of shipping produced.

By the 1950s its shipbuilding tradition was centred largely on the fishing industry.

GOLDEN CROWN WY78 on the beach at Staithes. She had characteristic Whitby coble lines.

One of my favourite Whitby-built cobles was GOLDEN CROWN WY78 which in July 1953 arrived in Staithes from her builders William Clarkson (Whitby) Ltd.

Following village custom when a new coble came, she was welcomed by crowds of cheering people lining the waterfront.

She was built to replace the earlier coble STAR OF HOPE WY174 which had been wrecked in the great North Sea storm of January 31st when huge seas pounded the village and the Cod and Lobster pub was partly washed away.

With an overall length of 30ft 5in, beam of 8ft 6in and depth amidships of 3ft 3in GOLDEN CROWN was every inch a true English square sterned coble but I was fascinated by her particular subtleties.

She was of broadish build, and somewhat full at shoulder and quarter with a strong sheer aft, a pronounced tumblehome and a broad bottom, and her relatively deep drafts were set well apart.

She was half-decked forward, and her three-bladed propeller was housed in a raised ram tunnel consisting of a hollowness in the sweep of the planking between the drafts.

Full lines

Cobles built in Whitby and district have their own style. They tend to be beamy with full lines, a lot of tumblehome, and a good shoulder forward, and are fairly hard in the bilge and have a raised ram tunnel.

"We considered that a fuller sturdy lined coble was needed when motors got bigger" said boatbuilder Tony Goodall of Sandsend, near Whitby, who has built more than thirty cobles.

"A 30-footer with an 80 horsepower engine, say, has a lot of punishment to put up with. If she is too fine she will take off in a following sea and broach to."

"A fuller coble will hold her head up and surf along the top. Also the fishermen wanted a fuller coble to carry more fishing gear. So our cobles carry their fulness aft with a proportionally bigger stern."

Gordon Clarkson worked with his uncle, William Clarkson, before setting up on his own in Whitby in 1950.

"I went on to build cobles bigger and heavier than anyone else at the time" he said.

"Engines were getting more powerful and cobles needed more beam."

Built in 1957 SEA HARVEST WY115 was still fishing out of Whitby in 1998. Note the fulness at her shoulders.

"I started the trend with beamier cobles such as SEA HARVEST with her fulness carried forward and a beam of 9ft 6in."

"I got a lot of orders as a result of building SEA HARVEST. I was never short of orders for the rest of my working life."

Built in 1957 for Skipper David Peart, SEA HARVEST WY115 was 32ft 6in long overall. In 1998 she was fishing out of Whitby under David's nephew, Skipper Robert Peart.

David said he likes cobles because they can be worked by two men and are economical to run and can do different types of fishing such as potting, longlining and salmon netting.

SEA HARVEST's tumblehome is formed by the top two strakes. Gordon said "A good tumblehome serves to tuck your knees under when hauling pots or salmon nets and stops you from toppling out."

Buxom

In 1973 Gordon built the beamy curvacious 30ft full-lined coble ENDURANCE WY89 for Staithes.

The purpose of her buxom shape was to produce a roomy coble within an overall length of 30ft and which was small enough to be handled up the beck by two men and would not occupy too much space at the moorings.

"With ENDURANCE we tried to give her owner, Arthur England, as much coble as possible, a good carrying coble, within her 30ft length" said Gordon.

"She is about the ultimate in fulness; any more and you would lose ease of handling."

ENDURANCE WY89 in the beck at Staithes at low tide. She had curvacious lines but a trim stern.

Despite her fulness ENDURANCE had a trim stern. Gordon said "Cobles move astern when hauling pots so the fishermen don't want a stern as wide as a barn door as it would cause resistance in the water. Also the sea would pick a wide sterned coble up and chuck her around".

Some of Gordon's cobles were slighter. Whitby skipper Louis Breckon who had the 33ft ALLIANCE WY39 built in 1971 made a speciality of longline fishing and believed that a finer lined coble was easier to handle.

Louis said "She had a tight turn and she held her head up well".

Raised ram tunnel

Gordon's uncle, William Clarkson, originated the raised ram tunnel in the 1930s.

It replaced the box tunnel which had been made by cutting a rectangle in the planks between the drafts and fixing a box-like structure over it to accommodate the propeller and protect it from damage when the coble took the ground.

"With the bigger horsepower engines these were not efficient, they were froth boxes. The propeller was like an egg whisk going round" said Gordon.

"It seemed unnatural to plank a coble's bottom and then cut a piece out for the tunnel".

The raised ram tunnel is formed when building the coble, firstly bending the ram plank into a long raised curve and then planking outwards and downwards towards the turn of the bilge.

"It is a natural steam bent shape, a gentle curve and, inside, the floors are shaped to fit over it" said Gordon. "Everything is smooth and easy and the water flow good with less cavitation and a more efficient drive".

William Clarkson formed the early tunnels with three planks between the ram and the rising strake. Gordon later used five planks producing a less severe shape.

As a result the sandstroke did not slope so steeply and required less bevel on its inboard face where it was fastened to the ram plank. This enabled the fastening to be stronger and more secure.

Half decks and wheelhouses

Strongly built half decks also became popular in Whitby for housing the engine.

The cobles were sufficiently full forward to carry the additional weight of the decks without going down by the head.

William Clarkson built the 31ft half decked coble GOOD FAITH WY97 in 1933 for the lady skipper and author Dora M. Walker.

Her book 'They Labour Mightily' tells of her career with GOOD FAITH and the doings of Whitby fishing fleet during the 1930s and World War 2.

GOOD FAITH was one of the first cobles to have a diesel engine. An Ailsa Craig 16-24 horsepower two cylinder model was fitted in 1934 to replace her $9\frac{1}{2}$ hp petrol motor.

Whitby fishermen were among the earliest to fit wheelhouses to cobles. The 37ft JANE ELIZABETH WY 144 built by the Whitby Shipbuilding and Engineering Company in 1960 was the first from a local builder with a wheelhouse.

Former yard manager Hugh Gollogly said that JANE ELIZABETH had a deeper forefoot and finer forward lines than many motor cobles to grip the water more firmly and keep her steady when working her gear.

Whitby boatbuilder Jack Lowther who set up business in 1961 produced some full lined cobles. The chunky 20ft 6in GUIDING STAR SH45, built around 1980 shows this well.

"She's beamy with a big pair of shoulders so that the engine could go further forward leaving more room aft, but she has a fine entry" said Jack.

I was charmed by a larger full-shouldered Lowther coble the 30ft DEEP HARMONY H WY51 built for Filey owners in the 1970s but fishing from Whitby during the 1990s under Skipper Harry Hoggarth.

With a canvas cuddy for protection forward, and

JANE ELIZABETH WY144 was one of the first Whitby cobles to have a wheelhouse.

DEEP HARMONY H WY51 was a full shouldered coble.

hung about with floats and fenders she looked like a waterborne Faberge egg.

The 30ft PILOT ME B WY216 built by Jack for Skipper Bill Blackwell of Staithes in 1975 was slimmer forward than the characteristic Whitby coble.

Bill told me "I asked for a finer bow to cut through the water more cleanly when going into the wind and so that she would not bounce up and down so much".

Sorts and sizes

The builders have developed various sorts and sizes of coble to meet conditions and requirements at their home ports or landing beaches.

At Redcar, a busy holiday resort near the mouth of the industrial river Tees, cobles work from the sandy beach.

PILOT ME B WY216 preparing for the potting season.

Tractors haul them stern first up the beach on two-wheeled trailers fitted with drawbars.

"These Redcar cobles must not be too big and heavy as there is some manhandling involved" said Tony Goodall.

"They need to be handy with smaller drafts and able to be launched and recovered quickly".

"It is important that their drafts are parallel and vertical so that they will travel freely onto the axle without causing stress to the hull".

In 1984 Tony built GENTLE BARBARA 11 WY17 for Skipper Ernest Thomas. Full bodied and eyesweet she was 30ft long with a 9ft 10in beam. Her 80hp and 2600rpm engine drove through a 1.5:1 reduction gearbox to a 19in diameter propeller which was small enough to fit between the drafts and avoid being damaged when the coble was ashore.

GENTLE BARBARA 11 had the full lined Whitby

looks but the 27ft SUVERA MH276 built by Tony in 1978 for Skipper Paul Wilson was a pretty little thing with leaner lines and 8ft 4in beam.

Paul was very pleased with her. "She's small and light enough to get in and out of the water quickly" he said.

"The beach is soft so you can't mess about or you'll get bogged down".

CRIMOND H SH130 built by Tony for Skipper Jim Haxby of Filey in 1988 was also a beach coble but was an individual.

Her owners wanted a beamy coble for carrying gill and trammel nets so she had a beam of 10ft 6in with 29ft 8in length and 3ft 6in depth.

Her stern was more vertical than normal with an extra 2in framing to lessen the strain on her when dealing with the launching procedure at Filey where a tractor pushed the cobles into the sea.

Gordon Clarkson built numerous beach cobles.

"Their engines should be a bit further aft to give better balance for going onto the trailers" he told me.

"Redcar cobles should not draw too much aft so they are easier to launch off the wheels".

"And I always gave my cobles a beautifully rounded forefoot. If too low and sharp the forefoot would dig into the sand".

GENTLE BARBARA 11 WY17 goes up the beach at Redcar. She had full lines but was a handy size for working from the beach.

SUVERA MH276 had leaner lines than GENTLE BARBARA 11

Gordon also said that beach cobles were usually open, because half decks would make them too heavy for hauling up and down the beach.

Largest coble

Cobles built to work from harbours can be larger than beach cobles, longer and beamier, deeper and more powerful with bigger tunnels and deeper drafts and more heavily constructed.

Tony Goodall's largest coble was EMMA JANE WY173, 37ft long and 11ft 7in beam built in 1987 for Skipper Peter Screeton of Bridlington.

Her engine produced a huge 130 hp to turn a 25in propeller through a 2:1 reduction gearbox.

These harbour cobles can have bigger slower-turning propellers which are more efficient and give a greater towing capability for working small trawls if need be.

CHARISMA WY313 built by Tony at a cost of some £30,000 in 1989 for Skiper Shaun Elwick of Whitby was also a big robust coble with length of 32ft 8in and 11ft 1 1/2in beam.

EMMA JANE and CHARISMA have wheelhouses but some fishermen preferred a simpler life.

Whitby Skipper Martin Hopper chose not to have a wheelhouse in the 32ft 7in half decked COURAGE WY151 which Tony built in 1986.

These stalwart modern cobles make GOLDEN CROWN appear quite small in comparison but she defiinitely showed the beginnings of the Whitby shape.

EMMA JANE WY173 was 37ft long and built for working from a harbour. She is being steered from the wheelhouse.

2. A CLOSER LOOK AT SOME COBLES

GOLDEN CROWN was one of three cobles built for Staithes in the early 1950s with financial assistance in the form of grants and loans from the White Fish Authority which had been set up in 1951 to re-organise, develop and regulate the white fish industry.

Since the close of World War 2, fishing from Staithes had been at a low ebb and in 1950 only the 22-year old coble STAR OF HOPE and one or two small boats worked crab and lobster pots between March and November and stayed ashore for the rest of the year.

The availability of secure jobs particulary in the nearby steel and chemical industries offered attractive alternatives to the uncertainties of catching fish.

There was a new interest in fishing as the 1950s progressed, stimulated in part by the Government finance which helped fishermen buy new boats and engines.

GOLDEN CROWN was built for Richard, Matthew and Francis Verrill. She was highly thought of as a grand little seaboat and was good at running before the wind.

Her deep drafts gripped the water and her relatively full shoulders prevented her from dropping her head.

During the winter she fished with longlines, catching chiefly cod and skate, and at other times she worked 150 crab and lobster pots.

She was powered by a Petter 10hp two cylinder diesel engine. Specially produced for fishing boats the Petter engine was robust and trustworthy and easily started. There were big advances in the design and manufacture of small diesel engines after World War 2.

GOLDEN CROWN WY78 taking crab and lobster pots to sea. Built in 1953 she fished from Staithes for about ten years.

On board GOLDEN CROWN a Hyland capstan for hauling pots was positioned on a thwart aft.

The hauler motor was powered hydraulically from a pump driven from the engine. Pump and motor were linked by two pipes. Pulling speed and the direction of the hauler rotation could be changed by means of control valves.

GOLDEN CROWN was sold away from Staithes in the early 1960s following the untimely death of Richard (Titch) Verrill.

Extraordinary heights

During the 1970s the first-sale price of fish reached extraordinary heights and British fishermen enjoyed big earnings. Almost all species were in demand because of a greater appreciation of the nutritional value of fish and the general increase in the costs of other protein foods.

In 1973 the total landings of all fish species landed by British vessels in England and Wales amounted to 497,180 tonnes valued at £89,534,000 compared with 543,763 tonnes worth only £48,245,000 in 1970.

Even so, fishermen needed high prices. There was massive inflation in the early 1970s stemming largely from the increasing price of oil

Fuel prices trebled between 1973 and 1974 and the cost of operating boats and buying fishing gear rose alarmingly. But the rate of inflation eased down as the decade progressed.

The demand for fish continued to rise and by 1977 492,154 tonnes put ashore in England Wales by UK boats fetched an astonishing £130,109,000.

The growing demand for quality white fish and shellfish led to a huge investment in inshore boats which were classed as those less than 80ft in Registered Length.

This increase in fishing effort also reflected the general expansion of Britain's coastal fisheries following the extension of territorial limits from three to twelve miles in 1964 and the good financial returns enjoyed by inshore fishermen during the 1970s encouraged young men to leave other occupations and go fishing.

Coble fishermen benefited hugely from the high demand for lobsters in Britain and Europe, and the marketing side improved with lobsters stored alive ashore in large tanks, using pumped seawater, to await collection.

In 1972 Staithes was the tenth highest port in England and Wales for the weight of lobsters put ashore.

Full bodied

Boatbuilders in Whitby and Sandsend provided the village with some stout cobles during the 1970s.

Tony Goodall built the 28ft 6in OCEAN QUEEN WY35 in 1971 for William Harrison and Richard (Dickie) Verrill.

She was an early example of Tony's full-bodied broad shouldered cobles and his first built under the White Fish Authority's grant and loan scheme.

With an 8ft 9in beam, she had nine strakes each side and her scatlings were heavier than, for example, those specified for a 30ft Whitby-built coble twenty years previously.

OCEAN QUEEN's larch $7/8$in planks were fastened to oak frames $2\ 1/2$in and 3in sided and spaced 14in between their centres.

The older 30-footer had $5/8$in planks on frames generally $1\ 3/4$in sided, and spaced at approximately 18in between centres.

OCEAN QUEEN was undecked and a $7\ 1/2$in high washboard was fitted atop her gunwhales from forward to amidships. Her drafts, set $33\ 1/2$in apart, were 3in thick and 12in deep.

Cobles were in the 1970s more heavily constructed to withstand the forces exerted upon them by more powerful motors.

OCEAN QUEEN was powered by a Lister HRW3MGR2 water cooled and electric starting diesel engine which produced 44.25hp at 2200 rpm and turned the 19in three bladed propeller through a gearbox of 2:1 reduction ratio.

OCEAN QUEEN WY35 was an early example of the full bodied cobles built by Tony Goodall. Note the pulling-out plates on the after ends of her drafts.

The Marine division of R A Lister and Co produced in the early 1970s a range of nineteen engines from 6.5 to 138 horsepower.

A metal A-bracket supported OCEAN QUEEN's propeller shaft, just forward of the propeller in the tunnel.

A Hyland hydraulic pot hauler was positioned on the after thwart. She carried a Kelvin Hughes MS39 echosounder in a perspex topped box under the thwart.

Echosounders transmitted sound waves downwards from a transducer on the boat's hull. Echoes were returned to the transducer when the impulses passed through a medium other than water.

The echosounder could indicate the distance of the target from the boat's bottom by measuring the time lapse between the transmitted signal and the reception of its echo.

Seabed depth and contours and the presence of fish could be indicated in some readable form such as marks on paper in the recording unit aboard the boat.

Echosounders were in use aboard cobles by the mid 1950s.

Introduced in the early 1960s the MS39 was one of the first fully transistorized sounders from Kelvin Hughes and found a ready market aboard small vessels.

It was simple to fit and needed little electrical power.

Trawling

In 1973 Skipper Harry Hoggarth brought home his new coble DEEP HARMONY WY 86 from the Goodall yard. She was the first of several boats of the same name owned by Harry.

Not quite so capacious as OCEAN QUEEN she was 28ft 3in long with 8ft 7in beam.

She had nine strakes each side and had a Lister HRW3MGR fresh water heat exchanger cooled 44.25hp engine with 2.1 reduction gearbox.

The manufacture of compact relatively lightweight higher powered marine diesel engines for small boats was made possible by the use of higher revolutions and sometimes lighter metal alloys. But reduction gearing was desirable because the engines rotated too fast for an efficient propeller.

Large diameter slower turning propellers gave better control and manoeuvrability to relatively slow and heavy craft such as fishing boats.

Beach cobles often had 1.5:1 reduction gearing in order to keep the propeller small for good clearance when ashore but consequently they lost some propulsive efficiency.

Many cobles were by now carrying more machinery for hauling fishing gear and DEEP HARMONY had a Model 500 trawl winch and Model 300 pot hauler from North Sea Winches of Scarboorough. Mounted on a thwart forward the winch had two main drums each able to hold 150 fathoms of $3/_4$in circumference warp.

It could pull half a ton when the drums were half full of warp, at a hauling speed of 20 to 30 fathoms a minute.

Drum breaks and dog clutches were grouped at the centre for easy handling. The winch was 38in long and was belt driven from a layshaft at the forward end of the engine.

Positioned aft, the pot hauler was very compact as the motor was mounted inside the capstan and it could pull half a ton at a maximum line hauling speed of 200ft per minute. It was powered from the engine layshaft through a Dowty 300 hydraulic gear pump which had its own clutch.

Flexible piping carried oil to and from the hauler.

Echosounder

DEEP HARMONY carried a Ferrograph G500 echosounder in a box with a perspex viewing screen.

Introduced in 1971 the G500 became widely used by coble fishermen for navigation and fishfinding and pinpointing wrecks.

Echoes were presented on a moving 4 1/2in wide dry paper strip and showed seabed contours and the presence of bottom-feeding fish.

DEEP HARMONY WY 86 returning from a potting trip. She was also equipped for trawling.

Hard and soft ground could be identified because rocks showed as a double echo.

Dry paper had a long storage life before use and the echo traces were less likely to fade if not kept in the dark.

The G500 could make soundings down to 500ft in five 100ft range scales and was housed in a splashproof non-ferrous casing and could operate from a 12, 24 or 32 volt electrical supply.

DEEP HARMONY had a 12 volt alternator driven from her engine. She used 300 crab and lobster pots in five fleets and sometimes trawled to catch small fish for use as pot bait as this was expensive to buy.

On occasion she trawled for quality marketable fish such as soles.

Highest number

Staithes people remember Arthur England's coble ENDURANCE, built by Gordon Clarkson, for her particularly full bodied shape. Arriving only a few days later than DEEP HARMONY in 1973 she brought the strength of the Staithes coble fleet to six, the highest number since before World War 2. At 30ft with 9ft 6in beam she was on a somewhat larger scale than OCEAN QUEEN and DEEP HARMONY.

Although having similar beam to the 32ft 6in SEA HARVEST which Gordon built for Whitby is 1957 ENDURANCE was shorter and thus proportionally more beamy and she also had ten strakes each side rather than nine.

Cobles now had a beam to length ratio approaching three to one as compared to some four to one when under sail.

Greater beam and depth and fuller lines gave them the required additional strength and buoyancy to carry powerful engines and hauling equipment and more fishing gear.

ENDURANCE was powered by a 65hp and 2400rpm Ford diesel engine which turned a Newage propeller through a Borg Warner 2:1 reduction gearbox.

She carried a North Sea Winches 300 hydraulic pot hauler and a Ferrograph G500 sounder.

Clean lines

In 1977 Gordon Clarkson built the 30ft coble EMBRACE G WY278 for Staithes skipper George Harrison and his son Neil. Although having similar beam to ENDURANCE she was less bluff forward and her clean lines aroused favourable comment.

EMBRACE G WY278 coming into the beck at Staithes in the 1970s.

In the 1960s George had the 28ft coble EMBRACE WY207 built by Gordon and designed for beaching with deepish drafts to protect her propeller.

Her Petter two cylinder 22hp engine was air cooled.

No water cooling circuits were needed for air cooled motors so cobles fitted with them could fish in shallow water without risk of breakdown caused by weed clogging the water intakes.

These engines were also liked for beach boats as they could be started before the vessels were in the water.

The new EMBRACE G was larger and more powerful than the first EMBRACE.

Her Petter PJ3 water cooled diesel developed 33.75 hp at 2,000 rpm and turned the three bladed propeller through a Borg Warner gearbox of 2:1 reduction ratio.

By the late 1970s Petter manufactured a range of air or water cooled marine diesels from 6 to 45 hp. George chose a water cooled version for EMBRACE G because it stayed cooler in warm weather.

EMBRACE G was designed primarily as a harbour coble and was somewhat too big and heavy to work from the sloping sandy beach. But at a pinch she could be hauled ashore if the weather was too rough for her to get into the beck.

The line of her keel was carried aft along the drafts to allow her to move smoothly over the launching boards. Pulling-out plates were fitted on the after ends of her drafts.

Following beach coble custom a mark painted on the shaft coupling was used to check that the propeller had one blade pointing upwards and the other two at an angle.

If the propeller was at rest in this position it was less vulnerable to damage on the beach.

None of these cobles built in the 1970s for Staithes had the planked half decks because the modern diesel motors were more able to withstand the weather and did not require so much shelter.

Open cobles provided more space for carrying and handling fishing gear and the engines were boxed in for protection.

Landmarks

EMBRACE G used a Ferrograph G500 echosounder well boxed in to protect it from seawater. It was powered from her 12 volt electrical system.

George said it was handy in fog for locating wrecks and hard ground.

He told me "Over many years we had learned the position of these by the use of landmarks but the sounder gave us more confidence to find the grounds in hazy weather".

Fishermen traditionally found their position by landmarks. 'Licence peeping' meant that a headland known as 'Licence' was just showing beyond nearer promontories.

Noises were also used. In fog the sound of the steam train blowing its whistle before entering Kettleness tunnel helped the fishermen judge their whereabouts.

The cobles were guided into Staithes through fog by someone ringing a handbell on the breakwater.

EMBRACE G worked 250 crab and lobster pots in fleets of fifty and used a North Sea Winches hydraulic Model 300 pot hauler.

The use of durable strong rot-resistant synthetic fibres such as polythene for ropes and netting made it possible to stay at sea longer and work more pots than in the 1950s because the fishermen spent less time ashore repairing the gear.

Pots netted with sisal or manila twine had rotted and broken and needed frequent repair and maybe lasted only a few months.

The twine, which was tarred to help combat rot, was so harsh on the hands it had to be softened with a piece of fat bacon to make it easier to handle. The ropes to which pots were attached were also sisal or manila and needed boiling and steeping twice a year in a preservative known as cutch. Synthetic twine was in use at Staithes at the start of the 1960s, pots being netted with orange Courlene which was an exceptionally tough and durable polythene fibre.

Conventional Staithes crab and lobster pots were in the 1970s similar to those worked all along the Yorkshire coast and made of wood and netting with a slatted wooden base 24in long and 18in wide.

Three half hoops of hazel or cane supported the netting which was usually made from Courlene.

Two funnel-shaped 'spouts' or openings made of netting entered the pot from opposite sides. Bait was held in the 'bait band', a double length of twine stretched between roof and base and the pot was weighted by a stone or piece of iron.

The catch was removed through a door in one of the side panels.

The pots were attached at intervals to a single polypropylene rope, and the fleet was anchored at both ends and marked with flag dahns.

In spring and summer the pots were fished well inshore and caught many lobsters but towards the end of the year were taken into deeper water up to four miles offshore where they were less vulnerable to storm damage.

Parlour pots

Increasingly a larger more efficient 'parlour' pot came into use.

With four half hoops it was 12in longer with an additional section or parlour at one end which was entered through a spout from inside the main part of the pot. Lobsters tended to move into the parlour after taking some of the bait, thereby lessening their chance of escape and leaving the rest of the bait so that the pot continued fishing. Some cobles worked a fleet of maybe thirty parlour pots whereas others used a few mixed in with their conventional gear. George Harrison said the parlour pots paid off well particularly if left for a few days as the lobsters could not get out so well.

He worked a few with his earlier coble EMBRACE and then made more as time went on but continued to use some small pots.

Longlines were now made from particularly strong spun nylon in place of hemp or cotton.

Staithes cobles generally worked three or four lines, each line being 360 fathoms long and bearing hooks on 3ft snoods at 9ft intervals.

Lines were normally worked up to five miles offshore in depths down to 35 fathoms.

Strange things

Strange things happened to the longline fishery during the 1970s and many coble fishermen switched to trammel netting for white fish.

Early in 1977 catches from lines were abysmal and one day a Staithes coble had a catch of only three codlings from four lines.

It was thought that instead of taking mussel bait the fish were feeding mightily from shoals of sprats swimming close inshore along the Yorkshire coast.

By early 1978 trammel netting was taking off in a big way all along the coast.

Six Staithes boats worked the gear successfully and caught Dover soles, codling, haddock and ling.

There was greater fishing effort as nets were worked in the summer as well as early and late in the year.

The name trammel is said to derive from the French 'trois mailles' meaning three meshes.

Trammel nets consist of two outer sheets of large meshed netting and an inner sheet with smaller mesh. They hang vertically in the path of oncoming fish which swim through the large mesh and become entangled as they push the smaller mesh into a bulge through the second outer net.

Typically these nylon nets were each 30 fathoms long and 5ft 6in deep and the outer sheet had 17in mesh and the inner sheet 4in mesh.

Set along the seabed trammel nets were held upright by a leadline along the bottom and floats on the headline. Several fleets of net were worked and each fleet was anchored and buoyed.

Gill nets also came into use. Consisting of one sheet of netting in which fish were captured by their gills they were less bulky than trammels and easier to clean.

Easier

Nets were easier to work than longlines because they cut out the tedious time consuming job of shelling mussels and baiting hooks.

31

However, in strong tides the nets had to be fished fairly well inshore. Longlining did not die out as sometimes lines fished better than nets, fish taking the bait when there was a scarcity of natural feed such as sprats or herring spawn.

Early in 1979 at Staithes the lines were catching more than twice the quantity of codling than the nets. It became practice for cobles to work whichever type of gear brought best results.

So EMBRACE G worked pots, longlines and trammel and gill nets. She also had a licence to work drift nets during the summer salmon and trout fishery which happily came at a time when lobsters were casting their shells and were of poor quality.

During her first year George and Neil hauled nets by hand and used the pothauler to heave the anchors. Later EMBRACE G was fitted with a hydraulic Rapp Hydema hauler comprising a drum on a pedestal.

Other new cobles came to Staithes in the 1970s.

In 1976 Billy Clarkson built the 26 ft and 8 ft 6 in ALL MY SONS WY267 for Skipper Ian Baxter. Powered by a Mercedes 36hp water cooled diesel engine with 2:1 reduction gear she carried North Sea Winches pot and line hauler, Ferrograph G500 echosounder and Seavoice radiotelephone.

Billy Clarkson had taken over the boatbuilding firm following the retirement of his father William Clarkson Snr.

'You can talk to a coble'

Despite the growing acceptance of new boatbuilding materials such as GRP (glass reinforced plastics) during the 1970s, many fishermen still liked wooden boats and preferred cobles in particular.

Whitby fisherman Laurence Murfield was fond of cobles. He said "You could talk to a coble. She gave me the power to say that I was the boss. She had to do as I told her".

Laurie, who first went to sea in sailing cobles remembered hauling pots using a washing mangle as a winch.

At 26ft ALL MY SONS WY 267 was a smallish coble

Gordon Clarkson built the 31ft x 10ft half decked coble MAYFLOWER A WY201 for Laurie in the early 1960s.

Another fisherman told me "Cobles are known as good little seaboats so we just kept to what we knew... You can get hard inshore among the stones to work gear. You just push her off the cliff bottom with a boathook". In 1973 I visited Jack Lowther's yard when the coble FAITH L WY87 had just been completed and six more were under construction or on order.

Built for Michael Locker who was then Whitby's youngest skipper FAITH L measured 34ft 6in long with 10ft 6in beam and had 44.25hp Lister HRW3MGR engine with 2:1 reduction gear.

A short marine plywood deck was fitted forward. Marine plywood is composed of high quality hardwoods bonded together with resin glue and is resistant to cracking and shrinking.

Tricky launch

Launches from Jack's yard were a bit tricky.

Situated alongside Spital Beck which was named after a hospital which stood there in the Middle Ages, the yard had no frontage to the main river.

Cobles were launched slantways into 5ft of water and had to pass under two bridges to reach the river Esk.

I was at the launch of the 33ft coble SHEILA L WY 191 built for Whitby skipper Arnold Locker in 1975.

Her motor was a Mercedes four cylinder 80hp diesel with 2:1 reduction gear and 22in x 14in propeller.

A Model MHN pot hauler from A W Smallwood Ltd of Bridlington was powered by a variable speed clutchless hydraulic pump driven off the engine crankshaft.

SHEILA L WY191 beining launched from Jack Lowther's yard into the Spital Beck at Whitby.

Scarborough trawling coble

Along at Sandsend Tony Goodall built some seventeen cobles during the 1970s.

Cobles were readily adaptable for inshore trawling and quite a number had small gantries to hold trawl towing blocks and cod-end derricks, and carried lightweight two-drum trawl winches.

In 1973 two cobles at Scarborough and two at Bridlington had made a living from trawling for some of the time.

The 34ft BARBARANN SH231 was equipped to fish in depths down to 40 fathoms thus taking trawling with a coble a step further.

A small wooden wheelhouse was set into the after end of the foredeck. This gave her crew some shelter and enabled them to stay at sea for longer periods. It also protected her electronic instruments which included Ferrograph G500 24 volt echosounder, Redifon vhf radiotelephone and Decca Navigator.

Invented in 1939 the Decca Navigator was a position-finding instrument which picked up radio signals transmitted from a group of shore-based stations.

The receiver in the wheelhouse gave readings which, when plotted on a marine chart overprinted with intersecting and numbered position lines, gave the boat's position.

VHF radiotelephones provided short-range communication in coastal waters.

The hydraulic steering gear had a removeable tiller to enable the deep coble rudder to be unshipped in port.

North Sea Winches supplied the hydraulic Model 500 winch and 300 pot hauler and the trawl blocks and sheaves.

The winch was modified to have larger capacity drums and carried 150 fathoms of 6mm circumference warps.

Biggish

A trawl gantry of galvanised box section steel was mounted aft and carried two open sided blocks from which the trawl was towed.

The Scarborough coble BARBARANN SH231 nearing completion. Note her wheelhouse and stern gantry. Being a biggish coble she had eleven strakes each side.

The trawl winch was fitted on steel seating bolted down to the engine bearers abaft the wheelhouse and the warps travelled round two sheaves on the after thwart and up through the towing blocks.

A tubular steel derrick was fitted to the gantry for hoisting the cod-end aboard.

Twin-tube fluorescent lights were mounted on the gantry and on the mast abaft the wheelhouse.

BARBARANN had eleven strakes each side. Double planking below the gantry protected the hull from abrasion from the fishing gear.

She was a biggish coble with 11ft beam and powered by a Lister HRW4GR2 four cylinder water cooled engine of 59hp at 2200 rpm driving the 23in propeller through a 2:1 reduction gearbox.

Morse throttle and rod-and-link gear controls were fitted aft and in the wheelhouse.

The Dowty hydraulic gear pump for winch and pot hauler, a Jabsco bilge pump and a 24 volt alternator were driven from the engine.

Normally cobles of this size had a 12 volt electrical supply but the greater use of more powerful lighting and extra electronic instruments called for a higher voltage.

Some 37 gallons of fuel oil were carried.

Lovely cobles from Gordon Clarkson in the 1970s included HANNAH MARY WY 84 in 1972 for Whitby brothers Alfred and Richard Wastell. Named after their mother, HANNAH MARY was 34ft 6in long with 10ft 6in beam and had a traditional laid half deck.

Beach cobles from Gordon included the 31ft KATHRYN AND SARAH SH 218 in 1972 for Skipper Richard Buchanan of Filey. Her Ford 65hp and 2000 rpm engine turned the propeller by direct drive.

The 30ft PROSPERITY H483 built by Gordon in the late 1970s for Skipper Richard Emmerson was heavily contructed to withstand unusual stresses when being hauled up or launched from the North Landing at Flamborough.

A Crossley single cylinder pertrol-paraffin engine hauled the cobles up the very steep slipway.

The hauling bridle was hooked to two ring-bolts which passed through the heavy stern frame of the coble and through knees fitted inboard between sides and stern frame

Also, the bases of PROSPERITY's drafts were flat and in line with her keel and forefoot so as not to snag on the slipway when she was being hauled ashore.

When the coble had been hauled up and the bridle removed, her weight was taken by two stout ropes secured to a ring on the slipway.

Each rope passed through one of the ring-bolts in the coble's stern and then around a thick strong mooring post at the quarter. During launching, the coble's weight was borne by these ropes and so the mooring posts were protected by heavy expendable chafing pads.

Gordon said 'This hauling and launching process knocked the stuffing out of the cobles.'

Also, the bases of PROSPERIYTY's drafts were flat and in line with her keel and forefoot so as not to snag on the slipway when she was being hauled ashore.

Some beach cobles were bigger. At Redcar the use of tractors and big axles with pneumatic wheels enabled quite large ones up to 35ft to be handled.

FREEDOM WY271 produced by Gordon in 1977 was 34ft long with 10ft 3in beam.

The following year Billy Clarkson built the 35ft x 19ft 9in AUDREY LASS WY291 for brothers Steve and Dean Dandy.

At Redcar some cobles are berthed on the Esplanade and AUDREY LASS often occupied the site nearest to amusement arcades and cafes and gift shops.

Her bunch of large luminous pink floats looked not unlike the balloons and candy floss carried by holidaymakers.

Other vessels sit further along the promenade or else in Fisherman's Square some 300 yards from the sea. Cobles and double-ended beachboats are often seen being towed along in a line of road traffic.

Busy and lively

Redcar had an extraordinarily busy and lively fishing industry. The development of small echosounders helped the fishermen to extend their activities.

During the winter of 1968-9 four cobles worked from two hundred to three hundred pots each, in fleets of fifty. Each coble caught some ten to thirty lobsters and eight to ten stones of crabs daily.

Echosounders helped the fishermen identify rock ledges and check the seabed profile and enabled them to fish for lobsters in winter seven to eight miles or so offshore in 20 to 25 fathoms, where there was little chance of pots being lost or damaged in rough weather.

They could also work trawls and use the sounder to spot shoals of fish.

During the summer of 1968 the 33ft coble MARIA

CRISTINA MH157 worked trawls and pots alternately. She left port at 4am and trawled until 9am and then worked the pots before returning home in the early afternoon.

Using the hydraulic pot hauler as a trawl winch she used small nets measuring 30ft 6in on the headline with otter boards 3ft 9in long and 50 fathoms of steel wire warp. She worked the trawl about a mile off in 10 fathoms of water and caught mainly haddock.

KATHRYN & SARAH SH218 sets off down the Esk following her launch from Gordon Clarkson's yard. She was designed to work from the Coble Landing at Filey.

Built by Gordon Clarkson in 1960 for Skipper Garry Mountain MARIA CRISTINA used a Kelvin Hughes echosounder.

According to season and weather and general state of the fishing as many as sixteen to twenty full-time commercial fishing boats and numerous part timers fished from Redcar during the 1970s.

Consisting largely of colourful clinker built double ended beachboats up to 23ft long the part timers generally worked pots in summer or took parties of anglers to sea.

Many men employed in the steel and chemical industries in the Teesside conurbation owned these small boats for recreational and part time commercial fishing.

Full-timers were chiefly cobles doing whichever job was most appropriate.

They worked pots, trawls, longlines, gill and trammel nets and salmon nets and ran an angling trip or two.

There was a big change to trammeling early in 1978 when thirteen vessels each caught up to 90 stone of fish daily.

During the late '70s trammel and gill nets took codling, ling, saithe, sole and turbot whereas trawls caught haddock, whiting, codling and plaice.

Most whitefish and shellfish are sold directly from the beach to local people and holidaymakers.

At Redcar the use of tractors and big axles with pneumatic wheels enabled quite large cobles to be hauled ashore. AUDREY LASS WY291 was 35ft long and had a wheelhouse.

Right: Low tide in early summer at Staithes in the 1990s. Five co[...] [...]d in the beck.

School at sea. The Petter engined coble *Federal Star* used by the Aden Fisheries Department to instruct Arab fishermen.

Below: Buil[...] [...]in coble GUIDING STAR SH45 was chunky and stout with big shoulders but had a fine entry.

3. THE 1980s AND 1990s: COBLES FROM SANDSEND

Decline and recovery

Reflecting the situation elsewhere in Great Britain, fishing in the Whitby area suffered from another nasty depression in the late 1970s and the first few years of the following decade. Demand for fish caught by British boats fell for several reasons including a huge increase in imports stemming from the rising value of sterling against other currencies.

At Whitby in January 1981 even best cod fetched only half the normal price.

. Profits from fishing declined or vanished, fuel prices went up, and there were weighty increases in gear costs and loan rates. Additional problems affected the cobles because crab and lobster catches declined miserably and in 1981 an increase in the minimum legal lobster landing size from 80 to 83mm carapace length caused a deeper collapse in earnings.

Things got worse.

By 1983 crab landings from Yorkshire ports were so shatteringly low that they accounted for only fourteen per cent of the English total as compared with fifty percent in the 1960s.

Lobster catches from Flamborough Head to the Tees had fallen by a third compared with ten years previously.

Overfishing was blamed and the lobster legal landing size limit was further raised to 85mm in 1984.

But the situation began to improve and the British fishing industry became more stable and optimistic.

After years of disputation the member states of the European Community agreed on a revised Common Fisheries Policy in 1983. The UK, which had joined the EC in 1973 was allowed to catch 37 per cent of the total amount of fish to be taken annually by member states within Community waters.

In Britain the Herring Industry Board and White Fish Authority were replaced by the Sea Fish Industry Authority with powers to develop and modernise the fishing industry.

It played an important role in promoting fish as a nutritious and enjoyable food.

There was a betterment in fish prices and the fleet's profit margins improved because of a drop in fuel costs and a slowdown in the rate of inflation, and grants from the Government and the EC gave a tremendous impetus to new boat building.

Nevertheless, there were new regulations and controls and Britain required that boats over 10m Registered Length carried Pressure Stock Licences in order to fish for species under quota restrictions although those of 10m Registered Length and less, which included numerous cobles, were exempt from individual quota limitations.

Many cobles fared well and catches picked up as the 1980s progressed. The majority of coble crews particularly south of Scarborough enjoyed their best lobster landings for many years and were heartened by signs of large numbers of immature lobsters on the grounds.

Quality codling was also in good supply with some cobles in 1987 catching sixty to a hundred stones of codstuffs daily from longlines.

More than anyone else

During the 1980s Tony Goodall built more cobles than anyone else in the Whitby area.

Gordon Clarkson retired early in the decade and Jack Lowther was busy building larger craft known as mini-keelboats.

Billy Clarkson had to vacate his premises in the 1980s to make way for road improvements.

Young boatbuilder Steve Cook, who served his apprenticeship with Jack Lowther, set up business on his own account in Gordon Clarkson's shed in 1983. He built two beach cobles but also produced mini-keelboats and double ended beachboats.

So Tony was the principal coble builder producing in the 1980s about ten from 28ft to 37ft long overall length.

The majority were designed to come below 10m Registered Length to escape the constraints of pressure stock rulings.

Owing to the way in which Registered length is calculated, using a measurement from stem to rudder stock, Registered Length and overall length are the same in a coble because her rudder is right aft.

Some of Tony's 1980s cobles are described here, and the building of his final coble the 32ft 6in INCENTIVE WY373 is covered in some detail.

HARBOUR BASED COBLE

SEASPRAY J SH237

Skipper Joseph Cooke, Newby, Scarborough. Completed 1983.
Length 33ft; beam 10 ft 11in extreme, 9ft 2in at gunwhales; depth 3ft 8 $\frac{1}{2}$in

Engine	C-Power 4/254 four cylinder 2722E Fresh water heat exchanger cooled 77hp at 2,600rpm,Borg Warner 2:1 reduction gearbox, 21in x 14in turbine propeller. Morse gearbox and throttle controls in wheelhouse and aft. Engine-driven Jabsco bilge pump, 35 amp alternator. Electrics 24 volt. Flexible mounts and couplings.
Haulers	North Sea Winches 300 Autoline pot and line hauler; hydraulic pump driven through clutch from engine.
Fuel	35 gallons.
Electronics	Kelvin Hughes MS315 50kHZ echo sounder, 17-27L radar and Husun 60 vhf radiotelephone from Kendall Marine Services, Scarborough.
Steering gear	Marol, from FRK Marine and Hydraulic Services Ltd, Hull.
Other	2 x 12 volt Lucas batteries, Whale Gusher 25 hand-operated bilge pump.

Designed for working pots, lines and trammel nets SEASPRAY J was a harbour based coble. Her engine was based on the new Ford 2720 or Dover introduced in 1982, which had the same dimensions as the earlier Dorset model but produced a bit more horsepower and higher revolutions.

SEASPRAY J SH237 was a harbour-based coble built by Tony Goodall for Scarborough. Note the platform over her engine, and her forward wheelhouse.

The 29ft coble PROSPERITY H483 on the steep North Landing at Flamborough. Gordon Clarkson built her in the late 1970s for skipper Richard Emmerson.

The colourful coble CRIMOND H SH130 built by Tony Goodall in 1988 fished from Filey under Skipper James Haxby.

Building the coble INCENTIVE WY373 for Skipper Adrian Turnbull of Redcar. Tony Goodall prepares the stem components to receive another plank. The distinctive coble shape can be seen clearly at this stage.

INCENTIVE WY373 was the final coble built by Tony Goodall.

Marinising companies

Since the mid 1970s inclement weather in the North Sea and the greater use of hydraulic haulers were causing cobles to fit more powerful motors.

Ford diesel engines have been converted successfully for marine use since the 1950s.

Marinising companies approved by Ford are provided with the basic engine ready to receive specialised parts designed, made or selected by the mariniser, including water cooled exhaust manifolds, bilge pumps, marine gearboxes and sterngear.

These conversions have considerable advantages.

Fishermen get a rugged motor able to withstand the salt water environment and available at an attractive price, and with parts readily obtainable as spares.

C-Power (Marine) Ltd was among some ten approved marinisers of Ford engines and it supplied motors to half a dozen Goodall cobles in the 1980s.

Tony said "We got to know people in C-Power's technical department and they were familiar with our needs".

Freshwater heat exchanger cooling systems are usual in coble engines. Seawater is pumped through a heat exchanger and cools the fresh water which is circulating around the engine. These systems are preferable to the alternative method of circulating fresh water through tubes on the outside of the hull. Such tubes would be vulnerable to damage on a coble.

SEASPRAY J's engine was mounted on flexible toughened rubber mounts, and a flexible coupling was fitted between the gearbox and propeller shaft.

These mounts and couplings are often fitted to cobles, which are prone to vibration and there is some flexing of the clinker planked hull particularly when grounding and beaching.

The flexible mounts help prevent engine vibration passing to the hull.

Tony said "If the mounts were solid your teeth would chatter and the wheelhouse instruments would also be upset. Flexible mounts can eliminate thirty per cent of the vibration. And you must have the flexible couplings to allow for engine movement".

Flexible couplings also absorb stress and movement should the propeller hit something solid.

Turbine propellers have rounded blades of adequate thickness to withstand damage.

Marol hydraulic steering gear was finding great favour in cobles with wheelhouses.

The wheel activated a hydraulic pump which forced oil at pressure along a pipe to a hydraulic actuator in the stern unit. An arm on the actuator would turn to port or starboard depending on which way the wheel turned.

The actuator arm was linked through horizontal rods and universal ball-type links to another rod which sloped up the inboard face of the square stern. The rudder pintle slotted into a square housing at the top of the sloping rod.

Thus the rudder would move when the actuator arm was turned.

North Sea Winches

SEASPRAY J's Autoline pot and line hauler, mounted vertically on a box base, incorporated a stainless steel V-wheel and capstan.

It was developed by North Sea Winches from the firm's earlier haulers.

A spring loaded arm prevented slack rope from dropping out of the wheel when pots were hauled in shallow water.

Rope was hauled more quickly and was fed down into the boat automatically.

Hydraulic power was from a constant delivery pump run from the engine, and a variable control valve near the hauler allowed wheel speed to be varied.

An open sided block on a davit enabled pots to be lifted to gunwhale level thereby saving toilsome retrieval by hand.

Access to SEASPRAY J's engine was gained from inside the wheelhouse. This was useful should the engine need attention when a load of pots was stacked abaft the foredeck.

The MS315 echosounder displayed echoes on dry paper 6in wide in a small but heavy duty splashproof metal case.

The sounder had a white line facility which helped the echoes from fish close to the seabed to be distinguishable from the seabed echoes.

Radar was increasingly in use aboard cobles and the Kelvin Hughes 17-27L was easy to fit and use. Scanning ranges from 0.5 to 32 nautical miles could be displayed on the 7in diameter cathode ray tube screen.

SEASPRAY J had a 24 volt electrical system rather than the more usual 12 volts. An engine-driven alternator, smaller than a direct current generator, fed current to batteries from where the power was available for distribution round the vessel.

SEASPRAY J later changed hands. In 1996 she perished in the interests of the Government's decommissioning programme whereby fishermen received payments in order to remove boats from the fleet, on condition the vessels were totally destroyed.

The scheme was designed to meet the European Union's Multi Annual Guidance Programme which called for cuts in boat numbers as a method of curbing overfishing.

LONGLINE SPECIALIST

COURAGE WY151
Completed December 1986
Skipper Martin Hopper, Whitby.
32ft 7in long; beam 10ft 6in extreme, 9ft 2 1/2in at gunwhales; depth 3ft 7in.

Engine	C-Power 4/254 Ford 2722E, fresh water heat exchanger cooled, 77hp at 2600rpm, PRM 2:1 reduction gearbox, Teignbridge Aquapoise '65' 20in x 15in three blade propeller. Morse engine controls aft. Engine-driven Jabsco bilge pump, 36 amp alternator. Electrics 12 volt. Flexible mounts and couplings.
Hauler	Spence Carter CL3 Capstan/Slave Line Hauler. Spencer-Carter hydraulic pump driven from engine through dog clutch. Remote control alongside capstan.
Fuel	30 gallons.
Electronics	ICOM M80 vhf radiotelephone.
Steering gear	Rudder and tiller.
Other	Whale Gusher 25 hand bilge pump. 11 planks each side.

Designed for working from a harbour, COURAGE was one of the few recent cobles with a traditional half deck forward and no wheelhouse. Steering was by traditional rudder and tiller. A small cabin with seating was arranged below deck forward. A hatch in the deck allowed for engine removal if need be. The radiotelephone was tucked under the deck's after end. COURAGE was Martin's first command.

He chose a half-decker because he had crewed on Skipper Brian Murfield's coble MAYFLOWER A for four years.

Martin said "I more or less copied her layout. She was easy to work. I just carried on with what I knew about".

The 31ft half decked MAYFLOWER A was built by Gordon Clarkson for Brian Murfield's father Laurie in the early 1960s.

COURAGE had 3/4in larch strakes on oak frames sided 3in and 3 1/2in. The half deck was planked with 1 1/8in Columbian pine.

The Aquapoise '65' propeller had a wide blade area and greater width towards its tips and was particularly suitable for cobles as the shape of the tunnel restricted the propeller diameter.

Maurice Brown, nearest, and Tony Goodall fit a plank onto the double ender FLORA JANE WY251 being built for Skipper Peter Lince.

The double-ender VALIANT STAR H73 coming ashore bow first at Redcar. She was built by Steve Cook for the Hornsea fleet but was later bought by Skipper Michael Haydon.

Staithes double-ender SEATON ROSE WY310 prepares to take pots to sea at the start of the summer crab and lobster fishery. Tony Goodall built her in 1979 for Skipper Frank Hanson.

Built by Steve Cook for Skipper Roger Thoelen the mini keelboat ROSE ANNE WY164 had very full lines and her beam was almost half her length.

COURAGE WY151 returning from a fishing trip. The half deck was unusual for a coble built in the1980s.

New Ideas

The hauler with capstan and vee-wheel was mounted on the after thwart. Morse engine controls and the hydraulic pump clutch were operated from the steering position

COURAGE sometimes worked some three hundred crab and lobster pots and also had a salmon licence but made a speciality of longline fishing.

Martin said "We've done well at the lines. The seasons are getting later and the winter cod has hung on longer. This year (1996) we kept going with the lines almost into the salmon season".

Working two-handed COURAGE fished four lines during four to five-hour trips up to six miles distant.

In the early '90s she fitted a Rapp Hydema semi automatic line hauler which dispensed with the tedious task of removing fish from the hooks by hand.

Incorporated in the hauler were two vertical rollers called strippers, placed close together to enable the line but not the fish to travel between them.

Thus the stripper held back the fish and pulled them off the hooks gently and without damage. The line travelled round a vee-wheel and coiled down into a box.

In order to work with the hauler the lines measured 5mm rather than the usual 4mm. The lines were rigged to improve catch rates. A swivel between backline and snood prevented the lines from tangling and allowed the fish freer movement when caught, and less liable to pull themselves free.

The snoods were monofilament and consequently more buoyant and less visible.

Each line carried two hundred wide-gap hooks which held the fish more securely. Research had shown that these hooks could improve cod catches by some twenty per cent because the greatest pullling force was exerted on the point and held the fish more tightly. Longlining was growing in importance for reasons of conservation and economy.

Automation reduced the fatiguing manual tasks. By 1996 some six or seven Whitby longliners were planning to use the swivels, monofilament snoods and wide gap hooks.

COURAGE used squid or whelk bait which tended to take bigger, better quality fish.

Some typical Whitby boats in the 1990's. The coble WINNIE S SN33 in the foreground was built by Tony Goodall in 1985 for owners in Cullercoats but later moved to Whitby
The larger boats in the background are traditionally known locally as 'Keelboats' to distinguish them from the part-keeled cobles.

PROVIDER AH71 was constructed by Mackay Boatbuilders at Arbroath in Scotland for Skipper James Storr. She is seen here on Parkol Marine Engineering's floating dock for a repaint. She was an ideal addition to Whitby's 'keelboat' fleet.

BEAMY BEACH COBLE

CRIMOND H SH130
Completed June 1988.
Skipper James Haxby, Filey.
29ft 8in long, beam 10ft 6in extreme, 9ft 3 $\frac{1}{2}$in at gunwhales; depth 3 ft 6in.

Engine	C-Power 4/254 Ford 2722E fresh water heat exchanger cooled, 77hp at 2600rpm, PRM 1.46:1 reduction gearbox, 15in x 14in propeller. Morse dual station engine controls. Engine-driven Jabsco bilge pump, 36 amp alternator. Electrics 12 volt. Flexible mounts and couplings.
Haulers	North Sea Winches 250 Autoline pot and line hauler, and 260 net hauler. Hydraulic pump driven through dog clutch from engine.
Fuel	25 gallons.
Electronics	Furuno FE-6200 echosounder, Navstar 2000 Navigator, Koden MD-3000 radar, ICOM IC - M80 vhf radiotelephone from A H Parcell and Son, Scarborough.
Steering gear	Marol.
Other	Seaglaze Marine windows. Electric bilge pump.

CRIMOND H SH130 during a trial run off Whitby following her completion in 1988. She was unusually broad in the beam.

Filey fishermen had a different way from those at Redcar for hauling their cobles up the beach. Each coble owned a pair of wheels joined by an axle but without towing bars.

The wheels were manoevred under the coble's stern and heavy concrete bricks were placed under the wheels to hold them steady.

Stopper ropes leading from the coble's after mooring posts were hooked to eyes on the axle. Chains attached to the tractor were hooked to the towing-out plates on the coble's drafts.

The tractor pulled the coble onto the wheels until the stopper ropes tightened which ensured that she was balanced correctly on the wheels.

Then the bricks were removed and the coble hauled out of the water. Before she was towed up the beach the tractor chains were unhooked from the drafts and hooked to the eyes on the axle. Thus the strain of towing was borne by the axle and not the coble.

When the coble was launched the tractor pushed her into the water until she floated off the wheels.

This launching process is tough on the cobles and their sterns are heavily sheathed to prevent damage.

Tractor driver Keith Crawford told me "We have four old farm tractors. The engines keep going but the outsides fall to bits. In a swell the waves can break over the driving seat".

Shifting sands

Conditions at Filey could be difficult. Filey Bay is shallow with shifting sandbanks and seas break dangerously inshore. When coming ashore the cobles can touch bottom a long way out and be vulnerable in surf.

Filey Brig, a long scar extending out from the Carr Naze cliff causes turbulence at its seaward end where it continues a further half mile under water.

CRIMOND H was carefully designed to withstand these circumstances and the launch and retrieval system.

Her engine was placed slightly further aft than normal. This distributed her weight further aft and helped

prevent her forefoot from catching the ground first and her stern swinging round when she was coming ashore stern first in rough weather.

Her stern sloped less than ususal to tolerate stress when the tractor pushed her into the sea during launching, and also enabled the rudder to be removed quickly when she was approaching the beach.

The rudder was designed to touch bottom simultaneously with the forefoot to allow her to get in further before the rudder need be removed.

Jim Haxby said "While you have the rudder on you are in control". Additional 2in oak stiffeners helped to toughen the stern. The drafts were an extra $1/4$in sided for strength and their bases curved up aft to move smoothly onto the wheels.

Tony Goodall said "Beach coble drafts are a compromise. They should be shallow for hauling onto wheels but deep enough to grip the water at sea and give better seakeeping qualities. We always left a $1 1/2$in clearance between the propeller and the draft bottoms for clearance ashore".

Jim Haxby liked CRIMOND H. He said "She's a good dry coble and runs well before the sea because of her broad beam".

CRIMOND H was particularly beamy for carrying gill and trammel nets.

She did some trammeling at the start but catches declined.

In the mid 1990s she worked 651 mainly four bowed parlour type crab and lobster pots in fleets of twenty-one on rocky ground from close in behind the Brig to five miles out.

Whelks caught in the pots were also marketable.

Working from three to seven miles out in winter she fished twelve traditional longlines each bearing two hundred No 17 hooks and baited with squid or mussels.

Jim said there was less fish on the grounds and expenses had gone up.

By 1996 the Filey fleet was down to seven or eight cobles compared with seventeen a decade earlier.

SOME MORE FROM SANDSEND

Tony built two beach cobles for Redcar in the 1980s.

The 28ft x 8ft 9in x 3ft 4in JANE MARIE WY337 delivered to Skipper Ted Price in 1982 had ten strakes each side as compared to nine for cobles of similar length built a decade earlier.

Ted said "She's a good safe seaboat. Cobles are sturdy and take a lot of punishment and bumping about".

Great charm

At Redcar each coble owned an old farm tractor which hauled her up the beach stern first on a trailer consisting of a pair of wheels joined by an axle and fitted with drawbars.

Launching and retrieving the cobles needed care. In the early 1990s one fell off her trailer and broached, damaging two planks and a draft, while being launched.

Another broached and was a total loss.

But some things had great charm at Redcar.

The cobles had Latin words or phrases painted on their sterns. That on JANE MARIE read LATUM TRIUMPHANTE which translates as 'Joyful and Triumphant'.

JANE MARIE was powered by a C-Power Ford 56hp engine and had a small marine plywood wheelhouse.

During the 1980s Redcar cobles worked at various times crab and lobster pots, gill and trammel nets, lines, trawls and salmon nets.

Cobles are adaptable and can fish for different species and switch quickly to alternative catching methods according to season and market and environmental conditions and the behaviour and disposition of fish and shellfish.

WINNIE S SN33 on the coble grid in Whitby for an overhaul. Her strakes had noticeable reverse curves forward.

51

In 1984 Redcar had a total of some sixty-five boats. Of these, thirteen cobles and six double-ended beachboats fished full-time.

Tony built the 30ft x 9ft 10in open coble GENTLE BARBARA 11 WY17 for Skipper Ernie Thomas in 1984. Shelter was provided by a canvas 'cuddy' erected forward. Her Mercedes-Benz 80hp engine drove a 19in propeller.

The engines of JANE MARIE and GENTLE BARBARA 11 were both fresh water heat exchanger cooled.

Air cooled

In 1985 Tony produced the shapely 32 footer WINNIE S SN33 for Skipper John Stocks of Cullercoats in Northumberland.

Should she work from a beach, her Lister HR3M 46.25 hp air cooled engine could be started before she entered the water. It also had the advantage of dispensing with water circulatng pumps.

The cooling air was suplied by a fan mounted on the flywheel. But air cooled engines tend to be noisier and their surfaces radiate more heat.

WINNIE S changed hands in the 1990s and fished out of Whitby with pots and nets for a while under Skipper Barry Tose before being sold back north.

Barry was pleased with her and happy with the air cooled motor. He said "There are lots of vents around the engine box and two on the wheelhouse top so air is well circulated".

WINNIE S was particularly full in the head and her forward planks showed prominent reverse curves.

She had the reputation of just throwing the water away from her.

Big coble for Bridlington

At 37ft long and 11ft 7in extreme beam EMMA JANE WY173 built in 1987 for Bridlington was Tony Goodall's largest coble.

EMMA JANE WY173 was the largest coble built by Tony Goodall. Here she leaves Whitby for a trial run following her launching. She is being steered from the wheelhouse rather than by the traditional coble tiller.

Skipper Peter Screeton wanted one suitable for working six hundred parlour pots some six miles offshore between Bridlington and Withernsea.

He said that 1987 had been a good lobster year with catches maybe double what they were three years earlier.

By the mid 1980s British fishermen were getting bigger prices for their catches and felt more confident in their future.

In August 1987 EMMA JANE was one of fifty-seven boats under construction or on order for UK owners with Sea Fish Industry Authority financial help. At 37ft long she was about the smallest. At Bridlington there was more investment in new and second-hand boats than for some ten years.

EMMA JANE had twelve strakes each side and scantlings were large in accordance with her size with $7/_8$in planks on frames up to 3 $1/_2$in sided and spaced 14in between centres.

Drafts were some 14in deep and 3 $1/_4$in sided. A broad gunwhale shod with galvanised strips protected the timber heads from abrasion and damage.

Her C-Power six cylinder Ford 2725E fresh water heat exchanger cooled 127 hp and 2600 rpm engine turned the 25in propeller through a 2:1 reduction gearbox.

She carried North Sea Winches 300 Autoline pot and line hauler and NF-3 trammel net hauler. Mounted on the port side the net hauler was largely aluminium to reduce top weight. Netting moved along a powered conveyor belt. Two rollers part-filled with water pressed onto the belt to increase friction but were flexible to allow fish to pass without damage.

The Model 250 hydraulic pump with remote control clutch was driven direct from the engine forward power take-off shaft. A flow splitter controlled the hauler speed independent of engine speed and a changeover valve switched power from one hauler to the other.

Hydraulic systems permitted flexibility in locating pieces of equipment because connections were made by flexible piping which was simple to install.

Wheelhouse fittings included Kelvin Hughes MS301a echosounder with white line facilities, Marconi Koden MD300 radar, ICOM IC M80 vhf radiotelephone and Marol steering gear. Electrics were 24 volt.

Next to the last

Tony's penultimate coble was the 32ft 8in CHARISMA WY313 for Whitby skipper Shaun Elwick in 1989.

Only 1in longer than COURAGE she was slightly more buxom with 11ft 1 $1/_2$in extreme beam and 9ft 9in beam across the gunwhales.

She had a wheelhouse, an 85hp C-Power 4/254 engine with 2:1 reduction gear and a North Sea Winches 250 Autoline pot and line hauler and worked pots, lines and salmon nets.

Shaun said lines were preferable to trammel nets as they could be worked in strong tides.

BUILDING A COBLE

INCENTIVE for Redcar

The 180th boat built by Tony Goodall since he set up business in 1953 was the stout 32ft 6in coble INCENTIVE WY373 for Skipper Adrian Turnbull of Redcar in 1992.

I follwed Tony and his fellow craftsman Maurice Brown through her construction.

Very few cobles are exactly alike in line and detail. Fishermen state their preferences in comparison to existing cobles but almost invariably ask for modifications based on their individual needs.

This brings about a subtle and continuous evolution in lines and proportions from coble to coble.

But those who know about cobles can usually recognise them as coming from a particular builder owing to certain qualities of hull shape and construction detail.

Adrian Turnbull wanted a coble similar to CHARISMA but asked for a greater beam of 11ft 3in and less tumblehome to provide more space for carrying gill nets, and shallow drafts for working from the beach.

Her fastenings were galvanised steel bolts, silicon-bronze ringshank nails and copper rivets.

Tony was asked to build her hull only. Adrian took her elsewhere for fitting out.

Maurice and Tony did not work from drawings. Various dimensions were predetermined, including length and beam, the depth at various stations along her length, the width and rake of stern and width between drafts.

Propeller diameter had also to be known in order to decide the depth of tunnel which, with the drafts, must give good propeller clearance when the coble takes the ground.

No moulds were used during planking-up. Hull form was created by using an existing set of plank widths, and angles of bevelling for the plank lands at stem, shoulder, midships, tunnel and stern.

CHARISMA's measurements were used but greater beam was achieved by increasing the width of one or two bottom planks, and a less pronounced tumblehome by reducing the bevel on the top two planks.

Peculiarities

The peculiarities of coble building began with the shape of the stocks which enabled her to be built at the angle at which she would float, with the deep forefoot lying lower than the stern by 18in.

This allowed all uprights to be established with a spirit level during construction.

The stocks gave the shape of the bottom of the coble's central spine.

Nowadays called the 'hog', the ram plank was the first thing to be laid on the stocks, steam bent into a long wave-like curve to form the tunnel's highest part.

Then the remainder of the back-bone was set up. More than 7ft high with one scarph the stem was temporarily secured at the lower end by a cleat onto the fore end of the stocks. Next came the 'swab' which extended from hog to stem. It was lapped over the lower end of the stem and the forward end of the hog.

Three strakes in position. Note the hog which has been bent to the shape of the tunnel. Also note the 'cow's horns' (left) which holds the planks firm during planking up.

The foreknee, reinforcing the join between swab and stem, was erected, followed by the apron which formed a continuation of the foreknee to the stem head and strengthened the stem. The stem components were bevelled and rebated to receive the plank ends, the precise bearding being cut out later as planking progressed.

Shaping the Tunnel

Six pairs of bottom strakes were fitted first.

The barrel shape of the tunnel was formed by planking outwards and downwards towards the bilge.

The sandstroke was an extraordinary shape, its outline swelling out to form the hump of the tunnel. To slope downwards it was bevelled on its inboard face where it was lapped under and fastened to the hog.

From a 45-degree declevity at the tunnel it twisted along its length to become a standing strake right forward. Abaft the tunnel it levelled out and tapered towards the stern.

Planking the tunnel requires enormous skill and produces one of the most unusual shapes in wooden boatbuilding. It aroused curiosity and prompted an American visitor to ask "Hey, fella! What's that great goddam hump"?

The second strake completed the tunnel while numbers three and four lay almost flat and five and six started the turn of bilge in the afterbody.

Forward, these six strakes formed the hollow lines of the entry and began the flare above the water line.

Planks were fastened by copper nails rivetted over roves in the normal boatbuilding manner.

They were steamed for maybe half to threequarters of an hour to make them supple. Nippers or 'tongs' were used to make tight the gap between each new plank and the previous one, ready for rivetting.

Planking up

At their after ends the bottom planks were supported by shoreing sticks and temporarily tacked to a curved jig nicknamed the 'cow's horns' set up on the hog.

The strakes begin to take the curve of the hull. After the 6th strake is in position the aftermost floor will be fitted and the 'cow's horns' removed.

This held them firm during planking-up and prevented them from straining the hog and splitting.

By the time strake five was in place, a batten representing the 35-degree slope of stern was nailed and shored up abaft the cow's horns. A sash-cramp helped to achieve symmetry during planking.

Strakes were in two lengths with staggered scarphs.

The strakes had 1in lands, with bevels no more than half the plank thickness. Bevels in excess of this would weaken the structure.

Bevelling varied in degree, being greatest at bilge and tunnel but non existant forward where the shape and run of the sandstroke governed the lie of subsequent planks.

To check for symmetry as each pair of planks was offered-up, Tony and Maurice used a device of their own invention, the 'inclonometer', to take angular measurements between the inclined surface and a spirit level.

Linear measurements across the coble or from the centreline were also taken with tapes or folding rules.

Most of the floors were fitted after six strakes were in position. Maurice drills holes ready for securing the second floor from aft. Other floors have been roughly shaped for offering up.

Staggered scarphs

Most of the floors were now inserted because they stiffened the structure before planking continued further, and it was easier to climb in and out of the coble at this stage.

The aftermost floor was fitted first, serving to bind the planks together so that the cow's horns could be removed.

Some floors continued further round the bilge than others so that when the side frames came to be fitted the scarphs would be disposed asymmetrically and not occur all along the same strake.

This produced a particularly strong hull.

Several floors were in more than one piece according to availability of suitable crooks but scarphs were well staggered. The floors were joggled and bevelled to fit against the planking.

An adjustable template nicknamed the 'dinglefone' was used to lift the shape of the floors from the planks.

Planking the topsides. The elongated-S shape of the plank is a typical coble feature.

Tony uses an adjustable template called the 'dinglefone' to lift the shape of the frame from the topside planking.

Silicon-bronzed ringshank nails were dead-fastened through the strakes into the floors. This was awkward work, particularly in the coble's afterbody where Maurice had to lie flat beneath the hull in order to hammer in nails while Tony held a heavy weight against the floor to keep it in position.

Planking the topsides now proceeded, strake seven completing the turn of the bilge in the afterbody.

The sloping batten was used as a guide for establishing plank lengths aft.

Transverse struts tacked to batten and hood ends helped to support the planks.

The two uppermost strakes formed the tumblehome. Owing to its strongly curved edge shape the sheerstrake called for three lengths of plank.

In older cobles, only the sheerstrake tumbled home as strakes were sometimes more than a foot wide with a fierce angle between them, and full-thickness feather bevels on some of the lands.

Modern motor cobles have more and narrower strakes forming a heavier stronger hull far less angular in section and avoiding the use of excess bevelling, and so

The topside planking is now almost complete. The temporary struts tacked to the sloping batten support the plank ends during planking up.

two strakes were used to get round the curve of the tumblehome rather than one

When framing was complete, all scarphs in frames and floors were through fastened from outside the planking by steel bolts.

Tony neatens a scarph between a floor and frame. Some floors continue further round the bilge than others for strength.

Distinctive features

Next, the larch inwires were fitted, running along inside the frames as support for the thwarts.

Extending 13ft from tunnel to foreknee the two heavy oak engine bearers were now positioned. A coble's engine is mounted forward in order to keep the shaft angle shallow to pass through the tunnel.

Next came one of the most distinctive coble features, the parallel oak drafts. Measuring some 18ft they were the biggest components in her structure.

They ran along the third strake for much of the way but their tops were joggled right aft where they crossed onto other planks where the bottom tapered.

Their bases were curved to enable her to move smoothly onto the trailer when coming ashore.

Each draft was cramped into place and holes drilled from inboard through floors and down through plank and draft to receive the steelbolts which were a foot to 16in long

It is customary to plank a coble's stern at a late stage in building her and this was done after the drafts were attached and the plank ends, originally left overlong, trimmed off.

The stern planking was stiffened by a vertical centre batten through-fastened inboard.

Other coble features including the stout outboard gunwhales were fitted. The gunwhales extended a few inches abaft the stern to avoid the final fastening passing through the very end of the gunwhale and causing it to split.

A heavy oak plank named the scutboard was fastened across the gunwhales aft, reinforcing the stern and pierced to take the rudder pintle.

Cobles are given a good degree of protection to their planking so oak listings were fastened below the top three strakes.

Stern clogs were scarphed to the after ends of the drafts and carried up the stern for about a foot.

They were through-bolted to oak pads inboard to take the strain of towing-out plates bolted to the drafts.

The stocks were now removed and the coble shored up on chocks.

Shaft logs

Because cobles have no sternpost, inner and outer oak shaft logs were through-bolted at the tunnel. The hog and shaft logs were bored to take the stern tube.

A removeable plate fitted above waterline level in the hog would enable obstructions to be cleared from the propeller when afloat.

Above: Local people wait to buy fish from INCENTIVE at Redcar. She was the final coble built by Tony Goodall.

The keel was fastened on last, extending on an upward cant to just abaft amidships. Its base curved up to meet the stem so that the scarph would be clear of the ground and not bearing the coble's weight when she was on dry land.

INCENTIVE is much admired for her beautiful and fair lines. Tony said "The tricky thing is to achieve the slight reverse sheer needed for a coble and to give the planks the required bend and twist and outline, running from the shallow bottom aft to the deadrise and hollow lines and reverse curves forward".

Left: Looking forward. Supports for the floorboards have been fastened to the floors. Note the removeable cover for the handhole in the hog directly over the propeller.

Square sterned English coble INCENTIVE WY373
Built by C A Goodall Boatbuilders, Sandsend, 1991-2

Length overall   32ft 6in.
Beam maximum   11ft 3in.
Beam inside planks at gunwhales   10ft.
Larch planking, oak framework.

Scantlings

Frames   3in sided, 5in moulded,
Spaced   14in between centres.
Planks $^3/_4$in sided.
Hog (ram plank)   1 $^1/_8$in sided,
10in moulded amidships and 7in aft.
Stem   3 $^1/_4$in sided.
Keel, drafts and engine bearers 3 $^1/_2$in sided.
Swab   2 $^1/_2$in sided, moulding tapering from 10in to
       2 $^1/_2$in.
Foreknee   6in sided,
Apron   4in sided, moulded 10in maximum.
Inwires   2in x 3in.
Stern frame   2 $^1/_2$ in sided.
Gunwhales   2 $^3/_4$in x 3 $^3/_4$in.
Scutboard 2 $^1/_4$in sided.
Washboard $^7/_8$in x 7in.
Mooring posts   3 $^3/_4$ x 3 $^3/_4$in.
Width between drafts 3ft 9in.
Extreme width of stern 5ft.

Fastenings

Through oak framework, galvanised steel bolts of various diameter, $^1/_2$, $^3/_8$, $^5/_{16}$in etc. threaded at inboard end and tightened with a nut on a washer, and some having square heads.

Planking dead-fastened into framework with silicon bronze ringshank nails. These have rings round their shanks which act as barbs to achieve good hold.

Planking fastened at lands with 2in copper nails riveted over roves at 3in to 4in intervals but leaving a gap at the frame positions.

Caulking at hood ends in way of stem.

Every component brush-treated with Cuprinol preservative during construction.

Rudder 10ft 6in long.
Tiller about 7ft long.
Propeller shaft diameter 1 $^1/_2$in.
Propeller diameter 17in.

Runs of galvanised bar fitted anywhere heavy wear was expected.

Larch and oak are traditional boatbuilding materials in Britain.

Oak is tough and durable and of ideal strength for frames and backbone components and can be obtained with a natural sweep of grain from which to cut curved members such as frames.

Larch is straight grained and abrasion resistant and moderately durable and often used for planking.

Barchards Ltd, the well known Humberside supplier of boatbuilding timbers, provided the good and generally knot-free oak and larch for building INCENTIVE.

The firm knew the type of timber Tony preferred for coble construction, using larch which had grown with a turn at the base, ideal for the elongated S-shape of coble strakes with the grain following the plank curves.

A page from Tony Goodall's notebook

In a notebook for future reference Tony kept handwitten particulars including basic dimensions, plank widths and bevel angles for each coble.

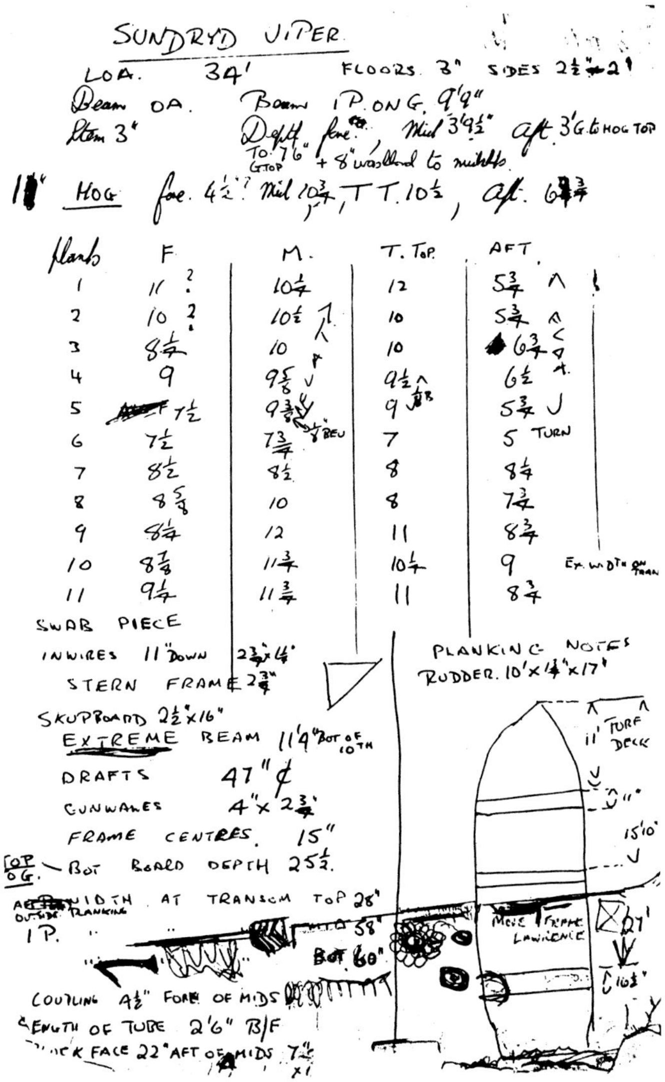

SUNDRYD VIPER.

LOA. 34'   FLOORS 3" SIDES 2½×2"
Beam OA.   Boam IP. ONG. 9'9"
Stem 3'   Draft fore. Mid 3'9½ aft 3'6 to Hog top
To 7'6"   G.TOP + 8" washbd to middle.

11" HOG fore. 4½" Mid 10¾, T.T. 10½, aft. 6¾

Planks	F	M.	T. TOP.	AFT
1	11 ?	10¼	12	5¾ ∧
2	10 ?	10½	10	5¾ ∧
3	8¼	10	10	6¾ <
4	9	9⅝ ∨	9½ ∧	6½
5	7½	9⅜ ∨	9 ∨	5¾ ∨
6	7½	7¾ BEV	7	5 TURN
7	8½	8½	8	8¼
8	8⅝	10	8	7¼
9	8¼	12	11	8¾
10	8⅞	11¾	10¼	9 EX. WIDTH ON TRAN
11	9¼	11¾	11	8¾

SWAB PIECE
INWIRES 11"DOWN 2¾×4'
STERN FRAME 2¾"
SKUPBOARD 2½×16"
EXTREME BEAM 11'9" BOT OF 10TH
DRAFTS 47" ¢
GUNWALES 4"×2¾
FRAME CENTRES. 15"
BOT BOARD DEPTH 25½
WIDTH AT TRANSOM TOP 28"
IP.
58"
BOT 60"
COUPLING 4½" FORE OF MIDS
LENGTH OF TUBE 2'6" B/F
... FACE 22" AFT OF MIDS 7½
×1

PLANKING NOTES
RUDDER. 10'×4½"×17"
TURF DECK 11"
11"
15'10"
10½

A page from Tony Goodall's notebook with details of the cole
SUNDRYD VIPER.
(Illustration used with the kind permission of Tony Goodall).

The adjacent illustration shows a page from Tony 's notebook with details of the 34ft Whitby coble SUNDRYD VIPER built in 1972.

Her name did not refer to a snake drying out in the sun but was an anagram of the surnames of her owners Purvis and Dryden. She was full and shapely with 11ft 2in maximum beam and 9ft 9in beam between gunwhales and was powered by a Lister HRW4MGR2 59hp and 2200 rpm diesel engine turning the 23in propeller through a 2:1 reduction gearbox.

In accordance with many cobles in the early 1970s she carried North Sea Winches 300 hydraulic pot hauler and Ferrograph G500 echosounder.

Fishermen almost invariably gave the builder their requirements based on an existing vessel.

4. DOUBLE ENDERS AND MINI KEELBOATS

Although the English square-sterned coble is the most celebrated inshore craft along the north-east coast, numerous clinker planked open boats generally known as 'double-enders' are also used for commercial and recreational fishing.

Many fishermen find them even handier than cobles for working from beaches and tidal harbours and creeks.

They differ from the cobles, being pointed at stem and sternpost, with full length keel, rounded sections and more and narrower strakes.

Measuring some 18ft to 26ft long they are lightly built for hauling ashore but nevertheless robust to withstand heavy breaking surf during launch and retrieval bow to shore and easy to handle when working fishing gear in lively water close to cliffs and rocks.

Remarkably pretty

The round sections of the double-ender are created by the use of narrower planks than those which produce the more angular form of the coble.

Double-enders can be remarkably pretty if their strakes are fair and eyesweet all the way. The plank edges at the overlaps are very noticeable in clinker built craft and help greatly to give the boat character.

Normally double-enders have slender ribs, known as timbers, which are steamed and then bent into place. The narrow planks and the shape of the sections enable the timbers to curve smoothly.

Clinker building is an old construction method and creates a strong slightly pliant hull which can tolerate heavy use.

Structural internal stringers are not needed because the overlapping planks add strength and can have smaller scantlings than those needed in a carvel built boat of the same dimensions, where the frames are set up first and the strakes fitted edge to edge.

Whitby builders have produced double-enders in large numbers.

One of them the 19ft MERINA WY19, built by the Whitby Boatbuilding and Repairing Co in 1947, belonged to my father. Tony Goodall and Jack Lowther built double-enders during their apprenticeships at this yard in the 1940s.

Double-enders are in great favour at Redcar.

Double-enders in Redcar. Their round sections are created by the use of narrower planks than those which produce the more angular form of the coble.

This little double- ender was built at the Whitby Boatbuilding and Repairing Co in the 1940s and was owned by the author's father.

PATRICIA CHRISTINE WY53 built by Tony Goodall in 1984 for Skipper David Marshall was a much admired example

Measuring 24ft long with beam of 8ft 9½in and midships depth of 3ft 2in she had C-Power 4/18 Leyland 110 Series four cylinder fresh water heat exchanger cooled at 33hp and 2500 rpm diesel motor set on flexible mounts and turning an 18in propeller through a Newage PRM Delta 2:1 reduction gearbox.

Her North Sea Winches 250 pot hauler and 260 net hauler were powered from an engine-driven hydraulic pump through a dog clutch.She carried 15 gallons of fuel and a Seavoice vhf radiotelephone.

Pulling-out plates were fitted at the forefoot for heaving her onto the trailer. Cleated iron strips along keel and drafts afforded protection on the beach. They could be replaced by undoing the cleat fastenings.

Bow first

Tony Goodall and Maurice Brown did much to develop the hull form of their double-enders to meet the changing needs of fishermen.

Tony told me "They are a similar shape at both ends and even better than a coble for landing through surf on a shallow beach".

"Although cobles have better seakeeping qualities they must turn round before coming ashore but a double-ender can come straight up to the beach bow first with her rudder in place".

"They are flat bottomed amidships and shallow draughted with sharp bilges, and the slightly rockered keel prevents hogging as well as improving landing capabilities when coming onto the beach and trailer".

"Shoulders and quarters are full for carrying capacity but we give them a slightly finer hollow entry to prevent blashing (slamming). Together with the slightly raked stem this hollow entry also gives us the chance to make a nice flared bow for seakeeping and a nice appearance".

"A slightly S-shaped sheer gives height at the shoulders where they take the seas first; the water comes up at the shoulder and not at the peak of the bow".

"Because the engine is aft they sit lower at the quarters (we call this 'boiling down aft') when under way so we give them more height aft than forward which also gives protection from the surf during launching and beaching".

"Some have a washboard built on aft to increase height but I prefer the gunwhale to be at the top because it is stronger".

"Strakes are narrower than those of a coble with a 24-footer having eleven or twelve. There is slight tumblehome at the top two strakes for seaworthiness and less top weight".

"The flat floors and low bilges and the drafts enable them to sit upright when coming ashore. Some owners prefer air cooled engines which can be started up before the boats get afloat".

Tony said that from the 1960s onwards there had been a trend towards these fuller heavier double-enders in keeping with the fishermen's wish to use powerful diesel engines and carry more fishing gear and hauling machinery.

And whereas a double-ender normally had steamed timbers, those built for full time fishing were usually framed like a coble with stout sawn floors and frames notched over the plank lands.

Come in

Dave Marshall of PATRICIA CHRISTINE said "A double-ender is a lot easier to handle on the beach. She can come in through almost anything and get as near as dammit out of the water but the waves pick a coble up and bang her down and everything shakes".

Dave told me that a 27ft coble could only carry forty lobster pots whereas PATRICIA CHRISTINE could hold eighty. This made a difference when pots were moved quickly into deeper water during bad weather to prevent them being damaged or destroyed.

"We use four hundred pots and work from close inshore behind the rocks to three or four miles out depending on conditions" Dave told me. "She's a good seaboat. We asked Tony to give her sawn frames for strength", he added.

Tony said "Dave Marshall understands every wave and how big it is going to be".

PATRICIA CHRISTINE WY53 on the beach at Redcar. A typical example of the larger double-enders built by Tony Goodall she is full at shoulders and quarters with finer hollow entry.

Redcar double-ender FLORA JANE WY251 was the last full-time fishing boat built by Tony Goodall who retired in 1995.

'Beam for your life'

In 1993 Tony built the 24ft double-ender FLORA JANE WY251 for Skipper Peter Lince as replacement to his coble which was wrecked on Redcar beach.

Peter said, "I've decided on a double-ender because a new coble would be too costly".

"My father and grandfather had double-enders. There's a lot of fibreglass and stuff about but we've always had wooden boats. I've asked for the same style of boat as PATRICIA CHRISTINE".

"My father said beamy boats were safe. He had a saying 'Beam for your life Give her plenty of beam'."

I visited Tony's yard when FLORA JANE was under construction. With beam of 8ft 5in she had ³/₄in knot-free close-grained planking cut from one huge slow-grown larch tree a metre in diameter.

Her 2 ¹/₂in sided sawn floors and frames were spaced 14in between their centres and made up from varying lengths of timber so that the scarphs were well staggered for strength.

Backbone and floors were oak but the frames were hard well-seasoned locally grown elm.

She was built at the angle at which she would float, with the heel some 5in lower than the forefoot.

Like PATRICIA CHRISTINE she had no washboard.

The hog was nailed on top of the keel before planking began so that the sandstrokes could be deadfastened to the hog rather than the keel itself.

This would enable the keel to be replaced if damaged.

Floors were fitted when five pairs of bottom strakes were in place and a coin was slotted into a floor scarph for 'sentiment'.

Fastenings comprised galvanised steel bolts and silicon bronze and copper nails as appropriate.

As with all Tony's fishing boats her scantlings were in excess of those specified by the Sea Fish Industry Authority.

Maurice (left) and Tony building FLORA JANE. Strakes are narrower than those for a coble.

She was built by eye, with a midships mould used only for guidance.

FLORA JANE had a reconditioned 36hp BMC water cooled engine with 2:1 reduction gear and carried North Sea Winches pot hauler and Spencer Carter net hauler.

Right for Redcar

In 1996 Peter Lince said "This size of boat is right for Redcar. She moves about more quickly than a coble at sea and we can get into shallow water for lobsters".

She did a bit of trawling for Dover soles, other flatfish and a few haddocks just behind the scars on the West Bay Soft and on a patch of soft bottom off Marske and Saltburn.

Trawl warps were 50 fathoms of 12mm rope towed and hauled by the pot hauler and the Vee-wheel on the net hauler. The net measured 24ft. on the headrope.

Crewman Paul Longstaff sometimes skippered FLORA JANE while Peter stayed ashore.

Paul told me "We work lines and gill nets in winter. Nets work better in a bit of a swell. We use six lines with three hundred hooks a line and squid bait".

"Squid can be kept in a freezer if the weather stops us using it straight away. Mussels are not so good once frozen. We go two to three miles off and get cod mainly".

Each of the seven fleets of gill nets was 450 yards long with 4in or 5in mesh and were left to fish overnight some eight miles from Redcar. In winter the nets were set on softer ground where the cod feed on sand eels.

During summer FLORA JANE fished 250 parlour pots in ten fleets around the East and West Scar but took them more than 2 ½ miles off if the weather turned poor.

Forty to fifty lobsters daily was a good catch. Lobsters were bought by wholesalers Tim Turnbull and Inshore Fisheries.

Tony Goodall had built double-enders for Redcar since the 1950s.

Early ones were finer at their ends with a less pronounced sheer and tumblehome, less flare at the bow and lower at shoulder and quarter.

They carried less fishing gear and were propelled by oars or outboard motor.

ANITA'S PRIDE on the beach at Skinningrove. She is characteristic of the double-enders built by Steve Cook.

Many had individual characters in line with owners' preferences.

In 1966 Tony built the 19ft x 6ft 4in LITTLE PAL MH2 for Skipper Bob Walton who could trace his family as Redcar fishermen back to 1740.

Bob said, "She was built on the pre-war style with less beam and a lot of sheer".

"My brother and I fished lines and pots full-time but now we work just fifteen pots for a lobster or two for ourselves. She was built for rowing, with her beam a third her length".

"The washboard was added when she was engined in 1967 with a Stuart Turner motor. Now she has an 11hp Ducati diesel".

"The big problem here is the size of the seas near to shore and if she comes through that you know you've got a good boat. She can't be faulted in a sea. She just seems to throw the seas away and doesn't care about it".

The largest Redcar double-ender in the mid 1990s was the full-timer 26ft x 9ft 6in VALIANT STAR H73 bought second hand from Hornsea by Skipper Michael Haydon.

Steve Cook built her in the late 1980's. Michael said "She's 6ft 8in high aft, higher than forward for taking the breakers when coming in".

VALIANT STAR had a Perkins water cooled 56hp diesel with 19in propeller and 2:1 reduction box and worked six fleets of gill nets for cod.

Steve Cook said, "My double-enders are full aft for lifting when the waves come and they draw more water aft. They pull and move to the fishing gear very well. They have a little bit of tumblehome and the keel is slightly rockered".

Outsize melon seeds

In Staithes the double-enders lie in groups of up to eight abreast like outsize melon seeds among a criss-cross of mooring ropes in the beck which flows to the sea down a narrow cleft between cliffs 120ft high.

Although in the late 1990s Staithes was still a working village with pots and bunches of floats stored on the quayside the full-time fishing fleet had shrunk to three or four including the bonny and curvaceous double-ender SEATON ROSE WY310

Built by Tony Goodall in 1979 for Skipper Frank Hanson and his son David she was one of the largest of her type to be produced in the area for some years and measured 26ft long x 8ft 6in beam x 3ft 2in midships depth.

She had sawn frames and a washboard and was powered by a Lister HRW3MGR2 water cooled 44hp and 2200rpm diesel with Borg Warner 2:1 reduction box and Spicers propeller.

A silencer was incorporated in the exhaust system.

SEATON ROSE had North Sea Winches Autoline pot and line hauler and 250 net hauler and a Ferrograph G500 echosounder.

Her $7/8$in planks were fastened on sawn and joggled frames spaced at 14in between centres.

Frank said that cobles were superior at sea but double-enders could come into the tidal harbour and beck bow first and were less vulnerable to damage when the beck was in spate.

Debris could catch against the underwater parts of a coble particularly between the drafts.

Frank had fitted SEATON ROSE with a home-made plywood windbrake aft. He said "It's a Godsend. It gives us a little bit of shelter and keeps the electronics dry".

TONY GOODALL RETIRES

The double-ender FLORA JANE was the final full-time fishing boat built by Tony Goodall who retired in 1995.

The 32ft 6in INCENTIVE completed in 1992 was his last coble.

Since setting up business in 1953 Tony produced 187 clinker planked wooden boats including more than thirty cobles and numerous double-enders.

Tony began his apprenticeship in 1945 at the Whitby Boatbuilding and Repairing Co which was busy with repairs and new buildings at the close of World War 2.

After two years as a shipwright in the Royal Navy serving with the aircraft carrier TRIUMPH and the cruiser SUPERB Tony set up on his own in the railway station coal depot at Sansend and built a 9ft dinghy.

His father Charles Goodall was the last station master at Sandsend on the Whitby to Loftus line which closed in 1958.

At the start Tony built small boats for visitors to Sandsend and did repairs for local fishermen,. He moved to another site on former railway premises in the late 1950s and remained there until his retirement.

One or two of his earliest cobles were only 20ft long. NIRVANA, built for Runswick Bay in 1969 had seven strakes each side and a raised ram tunnel. Her Ailsa Craig 10hp petrol engine drove a 10in propeller.

From the late 1960s onwards Tony experienced a tremendous demand for inshore fishing boats many financed under the White Fish Authority grant and loan scheme.

Tony said, "The fishermen have been excellent to work for. They knew what they wanted yet were open to accepting our advice. I've had a lot of satisfaction."

"I've been my own boss, my own judge and jury. All the boats have a character. I couldn't do with being pressurised into mass production".

On occasion Tony employed three boatbuilders including younger brother Leslie, and Ken Ferguson from Staithes, but fellow craftsman Maurice Brown worked with Tony for some twenty years. Tony valued Maurice's skilled help hugely and said, "He was my right hand man. We worked as a team".

EARLY MINI KEELBOATS

Towards the close of the 1960s Whitby's full time fishing fleet largely composed about a dozen cobles and twelve 'keelboats'. Mainly of Scottish build, the keelboats were so named to distinguish them from the part-keeled cobles.

All but two, the fifie sterned GALILEE WY68 and canoe sterned ENDEAVOUR WY1 had joined the fleet since 1957.

GALILEE and ENDEAVOUR worked crab and lobster pots. With a crew of five, GALILEE worked 270 pots in three fleets and fished up to six miles from port in depths down to thirty fathoms and spent seven hours at sea each day.

Five keelboats caught white fish using flydragging seine nets in the summer and trawls in winter.

Two trawled all the year round and three worked pots in winter and seines or trawls in summer.

The seine and trawl fleet normally stayed at sea for one day so Whitby fish was always very fresh and being well washed and packed in flake ice it was renowned throughout the country for its high quality.

In 1965 the Whitby Fishermen's Ice Society constructed an ice-making plant whch could produce ten tons of flake ice daily.

Flake ice did not bruise the fish and it also penetrated the gills and gut.

Landings of white fish, mainly cod, haddock, plaice and whiting had increased annually from 9,755 cwt in 1957 to 36,096 cwt in 1967 owing to the build up of this modern fleet of seining and trawling keelboats.

Herring were by now so scarce that in 1968 only one keelboat, OCEAN VENTURE KY209 worked drift nets for a few weeks, whereas during the 1940s and '50s the superabundant shoals off the Yorkshire coast made Whitby a major herring port and the base for over a hundred visiting Scottish boats during the season in late summer.

Caused a stir

Although cobles and keelboats continued to form the mainstay for Whitby fishermen during the 1970s the local yards began to produce another type of fishing vessel known locally as mini keelboats.

In 1974 Jack Lowther built the transom sterned clinker planked RACHEL CLAIRE WY142 for Skipper Robert Allen. She caused quite a stir being among the first mini keelboats to join the full-time Whitby fishing fleet.

She was seen as the possible successor to the coble, being roomier and able to work further afield in worse weather, carry more fishing gear and bigger catches and give the fishermen more shelter and comfort.

As she was fully decked, any water coming aboard would drain off, whereas if a coble shipped sea the water stayed in.

Although similar in length to a coble RACHEL CLAIRE was 2 ft beamier. With 33ft 2in length overall and beam of 12ft she had a draught of 4ft 6in aft to grip the water and could be worked by three people as against four or five in the 50ft keelboats.

RACHEL CLAIRE WY142 built in 1974 was among the first mini keelboats to join the full-time Whitby fishing fleet.

The concept of the mini keelboat had already been in the fishermen's and boatbuilders' thoughts for a few years.

In the 1960s Jack Lowther built the 22ft cruiser sterned SEA URCHIN for use by divers. Her owner had seen a small carvel planked cruiser sterned boat built by James N Miller and Sons at St.Monans in Scotland and wanted one like her.

SEA URCHIN however was clinker planked and had sawn frames every 3ft and steamed timbers in between

Later Jack produced a dozen or so similar boats 22ft to 24ft long for part time fishermen working from Paddy's Hole in the Tees estuary. He built the hulls only and they were fitted out by other people.

Built by eye they had sawn frames spaced 15in between centres and were full at bow and quarter with fine entry and forward raking stem.

Their buxom cruiser sterns had considerable tumblehome in profile. Jack had begun his apprenticeship at the Whitby Boatbuilding and Repairing Co in the 1940s when the yard was building voluminous cruiser sterned Danish type seine net vessels.

He later started his own business building sailing dinghies before moving into fishing boats and built his first cobles in the 1960s.

The cruiser sterned CHRISTINA P was one of the earlier mini keelboats built by Jack Lowther.

One of these Paddy's Hole boats the 23 footer CHRISTINA P was later bought by Whitby skipper Ronnie Frampton and was still fishing from that port in the late 1990s.

Ronnie said "I do a bit of salmon netting. She's a good little thing, a good seaboat. We were three miles off and it blew up a Force 8 and we just came along steadily. She handles nicely".

Ideal

RACHEL CLAIRE was the first mini keelboat to be built by Jack for a full time fisherman and was also his first with a sealed deck.

Robert Allen had seen boats of broadly like design in Scotland and Northumberland and felt that they were ideal for working pots and lines.

RACHEL CLAIRE cost some £9,000 to build as compared with £7,000 for a coble and nearon £60,000 for a keelboat.

Shewas constructed in five months by Jack and his employees Tony Marshall and Dave Winspear and apprentice Steve Cook.

Dave and Steve later went into boatbuilding on their own account.

RACHEL CLAIRE's wheelhouse was aft, and below deck she was subdivided from forward into cabin, gear store and engine room. She was powered by a C-Power six cylinder 2715E Ford diesel which developed 120hp at 2400rpm and turned a 29in diameter and 21in pitch propeller through a Borg Warner 3:1 reduction gearbox.

Owing to the design of the aperture the propeller could have greater diameter than that of a coble of similar length and taken with the 3:1 reduction gear, could produce good thrust for trawling if required.

A Jabsco bilge pump and 24 volt alternator and the Dowty hydraulic pump for the hauler were driven from the engine. Two fuel tanks held in total 120 gallons.

The North Sea Winches pot hauler with local controls was fitted on the after port end of the foredeck and the pump clutch could be engaged from the wheelhouse. Duplicate engine and steering controls were located near the hauler so that the skipper could manoeuvre the boat and work the hauler when working pots.

Wheelhouse equipment included Kelvin Hughes MS39 echosounder, Marconi Corvette radio telephone, K & L hydraulic steering gear and Furuno radar.

The sounder gave good ground discrimination which was useful for pot and line fishing and the radar was invaluable for locating dahns and buoys in fog and enabled RACHEL CLAIRE to carry on fishing when other small boats were fogbound.

A calor gas stove and seating were fitted in the small cabin beneath the foredeck and a mizzen mast with steadying sail was positioned abaft the wheelhouse.

RACHEL CLAIRE was robustly built with 1in planks on frames 3in sided, moulded 9in at keel, 6in at bilge and 4in at topsides and spaced 14in between centres.

Her wheelhouse was marine plywood on a mahogany framework with aluminium framed windows.

RACHEL CLAIRE worked seven longlines and three hundred pots. Her longlines were cotton which Robert Allen said fished better than those made of nylon.

The only one

Tony Goodall at Sandsend produced only one mini keelboat the 35ft 6in x 12ft clinker planked trawler CHALLENGE A WY133 in 1974 for the Challenge Fishing Company which was owned by Skipper Malcolm Stephenson of Bridlington and his Partners.

With transom stern and raked stem she drew some 4ft 6in aft and 3ft 6in forward and had fine entry but flared bow to give full lines forward at deck level.

The marine plywood wheelhouse was set into a GRP whaleback.

Much thought was being given to mini keelboat design. A similar type of craft the 36ft length overall and 11ft 10in beam RESOLUTION WY116 built at Amble in the mid 1960s had recently joined the Whitby fleet.

Compared with RESOLUTION, CHALLENGE A was given broader shoulders and her beam and depth were carried further aft.

CHALLENGE A was decked except for two wells 22in deep along each side of the deck from 6ft abaft the wheelhouse to 6ft forward of the stern.

Fitted abaft the wheelhouse the trawl winch from A W Smallwood Ltd of Bridlington had large capacity drums with flanges 2ft 6in in diameter.

Hydraulic power was provided by a Dowty variable displacement swashplate type pump belt driven from the engine. The rate of oil delivery from the pump, and hence the winch speed, was controlled by a lever in the wheelhouse.

A trawl gantry made from rectangular hollow steel section straddled the stern. Trawl warps travelled from the winch to towing blocks via leads mounted on deck forward of the gantry.

After passing through the towing blocks the warps were brought together and clipped to a towing post fitted on the centreline to give more precise control of the trawl when towing.

CHALLENGE A WY133 was the only mini keelboat built by Tony Goodall. She was designed as a trawler for Bridlington.

A steel derrick for lifting the cod end was fitted near the gantry.

CHALLENGE A was powered by a Lister JW6MGR2 six cylinder fresh water heat exchanger cooled motor of 138hp at 2000rpm with 28in propeller and Self Changing Gears 2:1 reduction gearbox.

It drove a Jabsco bilge and deckwash pump and 24 volt alternator.

Some 115 gallons of fuel were carried.

Wheelhouse fittings included Decca 050 radar, Atlas 240 echosounder, Seavoice vhf radiotelephone, Morse engine controls and K & L hydraulic steering gear.

Below deck CHALLENGE A had forward cabin followed by storeroom and engine room.

Her heavy scantlings included $1\frac{1}{8}$in planking on grown oak frames $2\frac{3}{4}$in sided and spaced 15in between centres. Deck beams were 4in sided under the winch and 2in elsewhere, and the deck planks were $1\frac{1}{4}$in thick. The keel measured 8in x 5in and stem 6in x 5in.

Steel knees and brackets provided extra stiffening below the winch.

During the previous ten year there had been a phenomenal expansion of Bridlington's trawler fleet.

In 1964 only four boats worked the gear but by 1969 the number had grown to thirty-two trawlers between 36ft and 60ft long.

In their eagerness to adopt this fishery some skippers bought second hand vessels of strange origin and character and fitted them for trawling.

Perhaps the most extraordinary was the 60ft steel hulled PENDONNA with narrow beam of only 12ft 6in and built as a steam pleasure yacht at Falmouth in 1901.

However by early 1969 ten purpose built new trawlers had arrived and four more were on order or nearing completion.

Differences less pronounced

Sometimes the differences between mini keelboats and full sized keelboats were less pronounced and some were carvel built to naval architects' drawings.

In carvel construction the frames are erected first and planks fastened to them and butted edge to edge rather than overlapping.

The 40ft 6in carvel planked transom sterned SHEILDENISE WY300 built by Jack Lowther in 1979 was more akin to the 50 to 60ft seiner trawlers in fittings and fishing capabilities but was also equipped for trammel netting.

She was built for a new company Streonshalh Trawlers formed by two Whitby fishermen Michael and Arnold Locker who formerly worked the cobles FAITH L and SHEILA L.

By the late 1990s cousins Michael and Arnold were directors of Locker Trawlers Ltd which owned seven Whitby keelboats up to 75ft long.

SHEILDENISE was powered by a Gardner 127hp diesel motor driving the 42in propeller through a 3:1 reduction gearbox.

Curiously, one of the earliest fishing boats to be powered by a Gardner engine was at one time owned in Whitby. In the 1918 edition of Olsen's Fishermen's Nautical Almanack I found her as belonging to the Esk Fishing Co and registered WY141.

Named GARDNER she was an 80ft counter sterned boat which had been built on steam drifter lines by J and G Forbes and Co at Sandhaven near Fraserburgh for Scottish owners in 1909.

A number of early motor boats were named after the engine makers. Gardner produced its first true diesel engine in 1928.

5. RUGGED MINI KEELBOATS

As the 1980s progressed there was enormous interest in boats measuring 10m Registered Length and under because they did not need Pressure Stock Licences and were exempt from individual catch limitations.

Registered Length is measured in a straight line, parallel to the vessel's waterline, from the fore side of the stem at the top to the foremost side of the rudder stock at the projected point where the stock passes through the hull.

Overall Length therefore exceeds Registered Length on the mini keelboats as the rudder was tucked underneath some distance forward of the transom.

A generation of small British fishing boats were designed and built to fall on or below the 10m Registered Length criterion. In some places one or two peculiar vessels appeared, with rudder almost amidships to keep the Registered Length below 10m and yet achieve the greatest possible overall length.

Whitby yards did not build these curiosities however.

Wholesome and rugged

The mini keelboats were wholesome and rugged little vessels built by traditional methods and based on well proven hull forms. Although as a general type the small heavy displacement wooden transom sterned fully decked fishing boat was by no means peculiar to Whitby, the mini keelboats further enhanced the port's notability for producing strong clinker or carvel planked top quality boats.

Mini keelboat SILVER LINE W WY68 ashore for a repaint. Note her transom stern, propeller aperture and clinker planking

The 34ft 6in (10.515m) length overall potter, netter and longliner SILVER LINE W WY68 built by Jack Lowther in 1988 was an attractive little full-bodied clinker planked vessel designed to escape the Pressure Stock regime with Registered Length below 10m.

Skipper Harold Winspear formerly fished with a coble but decided a mini keelboat would have greater range and versatility.

Basically an expanded version of RACHEL CLAIRE but with wheelhouse forward and carvel planked bulwarks she had 13ft 8in beam and 4ft 6in draught.

Her mahogany wheelhouse was set well forward to provide an uncluttered deck 22 ft long.

SILVER LINE W was powered by a Gardner 6LXB 127hp and 1500rpm engine which turned the four bladed propeller through a Twin Disc 1 $\frac{1}{2}$:1 reduction gearbox.

Her fittings included Spencer Carter line and pot hauler and Koden colour echosounder. Dual steering positions and engine controls were placed in the wheelhouse and near the hauler.

None quite like the other

Steve Cook built some 'hefty' clinker planked mini keelboats. None was quite like the other in shape. One of the advantages of wood for boatbuilding is that minor alterations can be made to successive hulls.

"They are general purpose fishing boats, able to do trawling, potting, lining and netting," Steve told me.

"They are very full beamy boats with full round bilges and a deep draught of 5 to 6ft which is a good stability feature and enables us to make a big propeller aperture".

"Propellers of maybe 36in diameter provide towing power for trawling".

"The straight stem is slightly raked. If it was too raked you would lose a lot of boat. They have a straight keel with a bit of drag and the floors have quite a bit of deadrise".

"They have a lean entry to cut through the water but a very full bow so that they don't bury themselves".

PRIDE & JOY WY218 outside the yard of Steve Cook Boatbuilders after a repaint. Designed to have a Registered Length of less than 10m she measured 35ft (10.6m) overall.

"They're built by eye and all slightly different. We set up three moulds temporarily just for guidance. If we are an inch or two out it doesn't matter as long as both sides are equal".

"We use the same moulds for each boat. To get more beam and fulness we don't pull the planking so tightly up to the mould. Six inches away from the moulds gives a foot more beam".

In 1988 Steve built the hull and superstructure of the 31ft 6in x 12ft 6in MARNY JEMMA for completion by her skipper Ernie Westcough from Teesville near Middlesbrough. Her Ford-based engine came from mariniser Beta Marine Ltd of Gloucester.

It developed 128hp at 2600 rpm driving through a PRM 3.1 reduction gearbox to a 31in propeller. MARNY JEMMA was equipped to work gill nets, longlines and white fish and nephrop trawls.

There is a vigorous nephrop fishery off Hartlepool. More commonly known as "prawns" and from which scampi is made, nephrops live in burrows on muddy parts of the seabed.

Next came Skipper Keith Wilson's potter and netter PRIDE & JOY WY218 in 1989 measuring 35ft x 14ft.

Lancing Marine of Portslade in Sussex provided her Gardner 127hp engine which turned the propeller through a 2.1 reduction box.

Trusting the eye of the builder
BOLD VENTURE 111 BH234 delivered to Skipper Michael Bould from Amble in 1990 was stouter than MARNY JEMMA and PRIDE & JOY and equipped primarily for trawling.

In the spring of that year Amble's fleet of some fourteen trawlers caught white fish and nephrops. Around twenty cobles worked crab and lobster pots or salmon drift nets.

Michael had liked the strength and shape and pleasing lines of MARNY JEMMA and PRIDE & JOY.

He said "I'm a great believer in looks. If it looks right you believe it is so, especially if you trust the eye of the man who is building her".

"Steve was willing to change things and let me have my say. I wanted her beamier with a bit more sheer, and a bit deeper both below the water and at the topsides, and with a wider transom for room aft".

"The engine is aft for quietness. High revving engines are noisy and make you tired. The cabin is forward and fishroom amidships". With Registered Length below 10m BOLD VENTURE 111 measured 35ft 6in length overall with 14ft 6in beam.

The bigger propeller aperture accommodated a 36in diameter propeller which, together with a 4:1 reduction gearbox gave good thrust for trawling.

Her floors were flatter and less hollow than those of MARNY JEMMA and PRIDE & JOY and bilges lower and fuller to give a generally deeper bottom and increased fishroom space and carrying capacity.

Michael was pleased with BOLD VENTURE 111. He said "She moves in the water well and doesn't dip her rail so you don't get solid water on deck. She has a big rudder and turns in her own length and is nice and easy to handle".

But he said clinker planking has some small drawbacks.

"The water is very noisy against the clinker planks when you're trying to get a bit of sleep. She's not too bad at towing but with clinker you get a bit more air to the propeller".

"Carvel planking gives cleaner flow to the propeller and you get a bit more bite. But in clinker building the builder can adapt and change the shape as he goes along".

BOLD VENTURE 111's layout was carefully planned.

The North Sea Winches GF30 trawl winch carrying some 175 fathoms of 12mm wire was offset to port abaft

the wheelhouse to leave the starboard deck area clear for handling static gear if so required.

The combined trawl gantry and gallows was positioned aft. Beneath the gantry the net drum, from which the trawl was worked, was offcentre to starboard to balance the weight of the winch. The net drum was driven by means of a cable, carried on a separate flange, being clipped to the port drum of the trawl winch.

This gave the net drum a powerful heave because it was worked from the trawl winch hydraulic power supply.

The trawl gallows were set inboard at the quarters to allow the otter boards to be stowed on deck against the bulwarks.

A forward-raking gilson derrick for lifting the cod end aboard was mounted high up on the starboard gallows so as not to use up deck space.

BOLD VENTURE 111 BH234 leaves Whitby for Amble after a repaint in 1996. Note the trawl winch abaft the wheelhouse. The large double net drum aft replaced the original smaller drum.

The landing derrick was stepped at the foot of the mast atop the wheelhouse.

The heavily galvanised steelwork on the vessel was fabricated by Lenny Oliver who worked with Steve. A native of Teesside Lenny served his apprenticeship with Jack Lowther and joined Steve in the late '80s and carried out all the steelwork on the mini keelboats.

He left and bought Jack Lowther's yard in 1993.

Steel

The woodwork on BOLD VENTURE 111 was protected in places vulnerable to chafing from the trawl gear. Galvanised steel sheathing was fitted along the toprail, and plastic cladding and convex galvanised strips on the outside of the hull where the trawl boards came aboard.

On the transom rail a length of plastic coated pipe enabled the trawl to be set away cleanly.

Internally, the outrigger and the half frames which butted against it were stiffened with steel to strengthen the after end of the boat and withstand the stresses of trawling.

A cod-end receiving pound and wooden prawn sorting tray were arranged on deck.

Abaft the winch steel hatches gave access to fishroom and engine room. Trawl wires travelled aft via rollers alongside the hatches and up to towing blocks on the gallows,

Fluorescent decklights on gantry and wheelhouse and atop the gilson derrick provided good lighting on deck in the interests of safety.

BOLD VENTURE 111 was powered by a Manta 180hp and 2600rpm six cylinder motor from Mermaid Marine Engines Ltd. of Wimbourne in Dorset.

Introduced in the late 1980s the Manta was most suitable for displacement fishing boats and was based on the Ford 7.8 litre industrial engine.

"It was designed to minimise noise levels and exhaust emissions whilst maintaining an exceptionally low fuel consumption" said Mermaid.

"Each engine is hand built to the highest possible standards and incorporates a special all-steel fresh water cooled exhaust manifold which eliminates the corrosion problems frequently associated with this vulnerable component".

A Jabsco bilge and deckwash pump and two 24 volt alternators were driven from BOLD VENTURE 111's engine. The hydraulic winch pump was powered from a power-take off on the PRM reduction gearbox through a Newage clutch and engaged by a Morse remote control in the wheelhouse.

Michael said this arrangement took up less space than having the pump driven from a forward PTO shaft.

BOLD VENTURE 111 carried 300 gallons of fuel.

The fishroom could hold some 45 to 50 boxes of fish and was insulated on the bulkheads with GRP.

The marine plywood wheelhouse had a stylish visor and Seaglaze Marine windows. Her JMC V-105 colour echosounder worked at 50 kHz for good ground discrimination and had a white line facility for better definition of bottom fish.

Also fitted were a Decca Navigator and RD80 radar, Husun vhf radiotelephone and Wills Ridley steering gear.

In summer during the 1990s BOLD VENTURE 111 fished for prawns and white fish as far as thirty miles offshore on the Farne Deeps.

Michael said neap tides were good for prawns and big tides better for fish.

In winter she worked close inshore some three to twelve miles off. Usually there was a heavy prawn fishery from September to Christmas and on a good day she would maybe catch 25 three-stone boxes of them.

But, said Michael "From Christmas to April anything goes. There is bad weather and not much stuff to catch so it is just a scrape".

The net drum was replaced by a larger double net drum mounted on the centreline, to carry a prawn net and a white fish trawl so that the boat could work whichever gear was required.

Each drum was locally controlled and had its own hydraulic motor driven from the winch pump.

"The drum is easier to control and we can swap from one net to the other in five minutes" said Michael.

In 1996 BOLD VENTURE 111 still had the Decca Navigator and JMC sounder but new fittings included ICOM radar and vhf radiotelephone, Robertson AP2500 Autopilot and Furuno GP50 GPS set.

Using signals from satellites, GPS or the Global Positioning System, provided position fixing with a good degree of accuracy.

GPS coverage of the North Sea was operational by the early 1990s.

Catch limits

In February 1990 a new ruling was introduced whereby the cut-off point for Pressure Stock Licences was changed from 10m Registered Length and below, to 10m Length Overall and below.

Consequently BOLD VENTURE 111 and also SILVER LINE W and PRIDE & JOY being more than 10m in overall length found themselves with individual catch limitations for those species subject to quota.

There was now a proliferation of new boats below 10m overall to escape the PSL regime.

Because fishermen wanted the roomiest vessel feasible within this length limitation some very beamy full boats were produced. Increasing the beam to length ratio in these small vessels was largely made possible by the use of the wide transom stern. The full beam sections could be continued aft with a resulting increase in deck area and carrying capacity.

Boatbuilders had a lean time in the early 1990s. A report* published by the Sea Fish Industry Authority in 1993 showed that the number of fishing vessels built in British yards fell from 502 in 1989 to only 219 in 1992.

The drop in orders was blamed largely on the restriction of building grants to the replacement of lost vessels which was introduced in 1988.

* A Review of UK Fishing Boat Building 1987/92.

On spec

Lack of orders led Steve Cook and Jack Lowther to build two under-10m overall length mini keelboat hulls in the hope of attracting buyers.

They would then be fitted out to their owners' requirements. Steve's hull was similar to that of BOLD VENTURE 111 but shorter to come below 10m overall length and consequently stockier at 32ft 8in with 14ft 6in beam and 6ft draught.

She had a wider transom and slightly more sheer aft.

Mini keelboat INCENTIVE BH243 was built under new regulations whereby boats of 10m overall length and below are not subject to individual catch limitations.

Skipper Geoffrey Burge from Amble was impressed by the looks and performance of BOLD VENTURE 111 and when he heard that Steve was building a similar boat on spec he moved ahead to get her and had her equipped to his needs.

Named INCENTIVE BH243 she was initially arranged for trawling but her wheelhouse was slightly offcentre to port so that pot and net haulers could be mounted at the starboard side should she switch to working static gear.

Completed in 1992, she worked from Amble for a while but was then sold to Scottish owners.

Carvel planked

Jack Lowther's stout little 'on spec' hull was 32ft 8in long overall with 14ft beam and 5ft 3in draught.

She carried her fulness well forward and aft but her entry was relatively spare to reduce slamming and throw the water aside.

Jack said "All my boats are full in the head. I built a dinghy when I was sixteen but she turned out finer lined than what I wanted. Even in those days I thought that a full boat was a good idea".

Carvel planking was used in preference to clinker because pots when being hauled could have snagged under the plank overlaps. Carvel planking is said to be more robust but not so lithe as clinker.

Her heavy scantlings were based on those specified by the Sea Fish Industry Authority for a 40-footer with $1^5/_8$ in larch planks on grown oak frames generally 3in x 7in and spaced at 15in centres.

Her deck was iroko laid on steel beams. Iroko is a West African timber able to withstand much wear and tear.

She was the last boat of any size from Jack who announced his retirement soon afterwards but said he might find it difficult to stay away from the yard.

He was still at work repairing boats a year later.

He said 'I've been involved with boats since I was twelve, when I built a canoe. Over the years the big development has been towards fuller and beamier boats".

Greater sea range

The hull was fitted out as BREAD WINNER WY367 and delivered in 1992 to Skipper Richard Marsay who formerly fished the coble CRYSTAL SEA WY296 from Staithes using four hundred pots in summer and gill and trammel nets and longlines in winter.

Providing greater sea range and fishing potential BREAD WINNER enabled him to work 1,100 four-bowed parlour pots in seventeen fleets.

Fishing from Whitby she caught as many as 300 lobsters daily in summer. She also fished some eight to twelve traditional longlines in winter and also gill and trammel nets.

Richard Marsay found that gill nets tended to catch better when cod were feeding and were lively and quick moving and got caught by the gills.

Trammel nets fished well when cod were moving slowly and not feeding and became entangled in the three walls of netting.

Later fitting a second-hand trawl winch BREAD WINNER did summer trawling for soles on sandy bottoms for a while and also trawled for prawns on muddy ground off Hartlepool in winter.

BREAD WINNER's deck gave 20ft 6in of clear working space between the forward wheelhouse and wide transom stern. Together with her beam which was carried well forward and aft the long deck enabled some 240 pots to be stowed safely.

The iroko toprail was $8 \frac{1}{2}$ in wide to form a platform on which to stand pots and was capped with two runs of galvanised convex bar.

Wheelhouse, foredeck and foremast were made of aluminium by Parkol Marine Engineering of Whitby.

A North Sea Winches pot and line hauler was mounted to starboard of the wheelhouse which was offset to port by 5in. An open sided block hung from a davit was used for lifting pots aboard..

A Tarbensen gill and trammel net hauler was fitted later.

Mini keelboat BREAD WINNER WY 367 was carvel planked. She was the last boat of any size built by J N Lowther (Whitby) Ltd before director Jack Lowther retired.

Cummins engine

Gill and trammel nets were hung between the steel flaking bars spanning the deck aft to be sorted and cleared of debris.

Below deck BREAD WINNER had forward cabin followed by engineroom and fishroom.

Mounted on steel bearers the Cummins 6BT 5.9M six cylinder 220hp and 2500rpm heat exchanger cooled engine turned the 30in x 26in three bladed propeller through a Twin Disc 3:1 reduction gearbox.

Cummins was the world's largest maker of diesel motors over 200 bhp with manufacturing plants in twenty places worldwide and more than five thousand distributers and dealers in 115 countries.

"The first successful engine we ever designed and built was for boats" said Cummins. "The B Series has up to 40 per cent fewer parts than competitive engines".

Aboard BREAD WINNER a 24 volt alternator and Jabsco bilge and washdown pump were powered from the engine, and the hydraulic hauler pump was direct driven off the forward PTO shaft through a flexible coupling.

Two fuel tanks held 300 gallons in total.

Served by a Hercules flush hatch the fishroom was insulated on the deckhead and held a hundred boxes of fish.

Her wheelhouse was equipped with Koden MD3600 32-mile radar, Koden Chromascope CVS-811c 50kHz colour echosounder, Decca Mk 21 Navigator, Sailor RT2048 radiotelephone, Seaglaze Marine windows, Marol steering gear, Morse engine controls and a calor gas cooker.

Images were presented in eight colours on the echosounder according to the density of the target.

For instance, a hard seabed was indicated in red. Dense fish shoals showed as red to orange and sparser shoals yellow through dark to light green.

Selected depths could be expanded for closer scrutiny.

Duplicate steering and engine controls were located outside near the pot and line hauler.

Cabin and engine room were reached from inside the wheelhouse. Three bunks were in the cabin which had 6ft 6in of headroom.

Electrics included three tungsten halogen 150 watt decklights and two banks of batteries.

A Faaborg hand operated bilge pump was also carried.

Whopper

In 1992 Steve Cook built the trammel netter ROSE ANNE WY164, a whopper of a mini keelboat with beam almost half her length.

Built for Skipper Roger Thoelen she measured 32ft 8in long overall with 15ft beam and 6ft draught.

She had similar shape to INCENTIVE but was even beamier and deeper to produce an exceptionally capacious and tough little boat under 10m length overall, with her fulness carried well forward and aft.

Her beam was only 1ft 6in less than, say, a 50ft keelboat built thirty years earlier.

Although arranged for trammeling ROSE ANNE could easily be adapted for other ways of fishing.

There was a well thought out reason for her shape and the choice and position of everything. The fishermen rarely want a standard vessel and give detailed attention to every aspect of a boat's design and layout and fittings.

Positioned on the centreline the marine plywood wheelhouse was larger than that of INCENTIVE and set into the after end of a raised foredeck laid with 1¹/₂in iroko planking.

Roger Thoelen was among the pioneers of small-boat gill and trammel netting from Whitby and many of his ideas on gear and catch handling were built into ROSE ANNE.

Her engineroom was forward to leave space aft for a bigger fishroom measuring 10ft x 14 ft.

Her transom was wider to give ample space for storing nets aft. The sides of the net bins aft were set inboard so her crew could stand on deck either side rather than on the nets when shooting gear over the stern.

There was also space between the bulwarks and the galvanised steel gantry to provide clear access for leaning over the toprail and retrieving the dahns.

For use during net hauling, secondary engine and proportional steering controls were set against the starboard bulwark from where Roger could clearly see the nets leaving the water.

A 100 watt floodlight on an arm mounted on the gantry could be swung out over the water to shine down onto the nets.

Another floodlight on the wheelhouse side directed good illumination onto the net hauler positioned at the starboard toprail.

The flaking bar was set 4ft above deck level rather than in the usual higher position.

This prevented debris flying in the fishermen's faces when they cleaned the nets, which were less likely to be blown about by the wind.

A small bollard on the toprail abaft the hauler was used for towing out anchors or nets which had become fast. Roger said "This is a little thing which we have found works well for us and the gear".

Mermaid engine

Mounted on steel bearers ROSE ANNE's Mermaid Manta engine gave 180hp at 2600rpm and drove the 30in x 22in four bladed propeller through a Twin Disc 3:1 reduction gearbox.

Two Jabsco bilge pumps, one for fishwashing and deckwash, were belt driven from the forward extension shaft on the engine.

The Dowty hydraulic pump for the hauler was powered from the shaft through a manual clutch.

The engine also drove one 12 volt and one 24 volt alternator because some equipment including the GPS navigator ran off a 12 volt supply.

A stainless steel 200 gallon fuel tank was fitted aft and the two banks of batteries were housed against the cabin bulkhead above waterline level.

Mounted to starboard of the wheelhouse the Sjovelar HF Icelandic net hauler, supplied by Marine Landing Services of Amble, was transferred from Roger's previous boat. These haulers were robust and lightweight with a tremendous hauling capacity.

An 8 stone capacity fish washer of Roger's own design was fitted to port of the wheelhouse.

The fishroom was insulated on deckhead and forward bulkhead. A raised steel hatch with aluminium cover, offset to port abaft the wheelhouse, gave access to engine and fishroom, and a flush steel ice hatch was on the centreline further aft.

Spare nets could be pulled up through the ice hatch and over the flaking bar into the net bins.

Six Aqua Signal twin-tube fluorescent decklights and the two floodlights were supplied by Northern Marine Electrics of Scarborough.

Galvanised steel protective sheathing capped the toprail at transom and quarters and extended down the transom edge.

Convex plastic strips elsewhere along the toprail and on the inwire also formed hardwearing protection and were easier on the nets than metal bar.

The hull was sheathed with Bexel plastic at the starboard side where nets were hauled.

Electronics included Marconi Koden Chromascope CVS-8821 50kHz colour echosounder, Kelvin Hughes MS605 back-up sounder, Koden 3600 radar, Koden KGP95 GPS navigator, Sailor RT144C vhf radiotelephone and Black Hawk radiotelephone.

A Decca Mk 21 Navigator was transferred from the previous boat and had a GPS-to-Decca converter.

Standing height

Other fittings included Wagner steering gear and Cetrek 721 Autopilot. Wagner also supplied the robust Kobelt engine controls in wheelhouse and on deck.

The wheelhouse had Seaglaze Marine windows and a stylish visor.

An aluminium H-frame mast and Rayline searchlight were fitted on the wheelhouse top.

There was more than 6ft of standing height in the two-bunk cabin beneath the foredeck. A small gas cooker and sink unit were in the wheelhouse and a 30 gallon fresh water tank was carried.

In compliance with safety regulations a gas leak detector and automatic engineroom fire extinguishing system were fitted.,

Other fittings included Whale hand bilge pump and M D Duff sacrificial anodes.

Fitted on the underwater hull, zinc anodes reduce corrosion between dissimilar metals. The anodes waste away rather than the propeller or other underwater metal fittings.

Up the river

Timber came from Barchards Ltd.

There was no road access to Steve's yard so deliveries of timber were towed there up the river Esk.

ROSE ANNE was robustly constructed of larch on oak with scantling similar to those of INCENTIVE.

Her 1in clinker planks were fastened on oak frames 3in sided and spaced 15in between their centres.

Frame moulding tapered from 9in at keel to 6in at topsides.

Keel and stem measured 10in x 6in and the hog 10in x 4in.

Deadwoods were 8 1/2 ins sided, apron 5in and transom frames 3in.

Half-frames forward and aft were reinforced with steel where they joined the centreline construction.

Bulwarks were carvel built with an oak rubbing strake at deck level, and an 8in x 2 1/4 in toprail.

The deck which measured 20ft from wheelhouse to stern was laid with 2in iroko on 6in x 3in oak beams fastened onto an oak beam shelf.

Both bulkheads were marine plywood but the after engineroom bulkhead was steel plate to half its height with a watertight gland to accommodate the propeller shaft.

ROSE ANNE used strong and durable plastic fish boxes from Allibert (UK) Ltd.

Designed to keep the catch fresh these had smooth surfaces to protect fish from damage and had external drainage.

Plastic boxes were by now used extensively in the fishing industry in preference to wooden ones.

Roger was well pleased with ROSE ANNE and said "She does everything we ask of her and there is plenty of storage space. She's a dry boat and stable, and she is quick in response".

"The whaleback (foredeck) keeps the wind off us when we're dodging into the weather on the autopilot and clearing the nets".

"She has put some weather away. We've worked the gear in a Force 8 gale gusting up to Force 9".

Steve Cook building the mini keelboat ROSE ANNE WY164. He is cutting the rebate into the upper edge of a plank ready to receive the plank above.

Gear technology

ROSE ANNE made her mark on fishing gear technology and fish conservation.

Late in 1994 she began trials organised by the Sea Fish Industry Authority as part of an international research programme to test the selectivity of various trammel and gill net designs and mesh sizes.

Roger said "My personal preference is for the $4^3/_4$ in (120mm) inner mesh for trammel nets because it doesn't catch many small fish".

"We work up to ten 400-yard fleets of trammel nets and get mainly cod with some turbot and plaice and lemon sole and a few big lobsters".

"Our nets are mainly from Selsey Fishing Supplies in Sussex with a 24in outer mesh and $4^3/_4$ in inners. We have had up to 120 stones of fish a day but normally average 40 to 50 stones".

ROSE ANNE's catches were splendid quality and fetched high market prices. Nets were left in the water for five hours or less so the fish were nearly always alive and in excellent condition when the nets were hauled and not damaged by crabs, seals or whelks.

Catch quality was carefully maintained. Roger said "After each fleet of nets is hauled we gut and wash the catch before hauling another net".

"We will also cut the mesh to disentangle a fish rather than pull it through the netting".

New rules

New rules came into effect to curb the expansion of the below-10m fleet.

From 1st May 1993 boats of 10m overall length and below required licences from the relevant fisheries department in order to catch fish, other than salmon and migratory trout, for profit.

These boats remained exempt from individual catch limits for pressure stock species though there was a collective quota for this section of the fleet. This could stop them fishing if the collective allocation for a particular species ran out.

New boats in this size range which had been ordered before a cut-off date in February 1992 were granted licences.

The mini keelboat ANDIGEE WY372 delivered from Steve Cook to Skipper Lee Guy in 1993 fell into this circumstance.

Designed to come below 10m length overall she was 32ft 8in (9.9m) long but, at the request of her owner was only 13ft on the beam with 5ft 2in draught so she was leaner and sparer than the portly ROSE ANNE.

The completion of ANDIGEE left Steve's order book for new building empty.

ANDIGEE was advertised for sale in 1995 and was eagerly bought by Skipper Kevin Henderson of Amble as replacement for a coble.

Kevin said "I've looked around for a year for a suitable boat with which to do a bit more trawling for prawns as well as working pots and gill nets".

"I like ANDIGEE. She's not yet three years old. Good boats are hard to come by".

Before leaving for Amble ANDIGEE was supplied with a net drum, trawl winch and gantry and her hull was sheathed at the quarters.

ANDIGEE WY372 sets out from Whitby with a deckload of crab and lobster pots. She was the last mini keelboat built by Steve Cook.

6. SCOTTISH BUILT BOATS AND OTHER INCOMERS

Motor fifies to shelterdeckers

In 1935 the new Whitby fishing boat EASTER MORN WY61 took part in the film 'Turn of the Tide'. Regarded as the best British film of the year, it was based on Leo Walmsley's novel "Three Fevers' and tells of rivalry between two fishing families.

Finally they settle their quarrels and go shares in a big new Scottish built boat of the type portrayed by EASTER MORN.

It was J. Arthur Rank's first feature film and shows splendid location shots of cobles and wild seas and the storm lashed Yorkshire coastline.

In the 1990's 'Turn of the Tide' was released as a video from Argus Films and the British Film Institute.

EASTER MORN WY61 approaching Whitby fishmarket. Her lines are reminiscent of the famous Scottish east coast sailing fifies.

Motor fifies

In reality EASTER MORN was built in 1935 at Anstruther in Scotland by Walter Reekie for Skipper Henry Duke and was a typical carvel planked fully decked motor fifie 42ft long overall with 14ft 9in beam and powered by a Kelvin 44hp 750rpm four stroke cycle diesel engine.

The type was descended from the Scottish east coast lug rigged double-ended sailing fifies which had almost vertical stem and stern, deep heel and forefoot and steep slightly hollow vee floors.

Motor fifies were generally smaller and not so deep with flatter floors and harder bilges, and the rounded forefoot gave better manoeuvrability.

They had a small wheelhouse and a mizzen riding sail and were powered by either a petrol-paraffin or a diesel engine.

With the arrival of the diesel engine, which was more reliable at sea and safer and cheaper to run than petrol-paraffin motors, Whitby acquired a small fleet of these sturdy economical vessels.

Locally named keelboats to distinguish them from the part keeled English cobles, they had sleeping accommodation, could make longer trips further afield, and fish in worse weather and deeper water and handle more fishing gear.

Herring fishing was at a low ebb after World War 1 owing to the loss of overseas markets, so the keelboats concentrated mainly on potting for crabs and lobsters and line fishing for cod, haddock, ling and turbot.

More than two hundred pots could be worked as against some 120 aboard the cobles, and late in 1935 EASTER MORN pioneered the use in Whitby of the Hyland pot hauler, driven from a hydraulic pump coupled to the engine.

Motor fifie GALILEE WY68, built by W & G Stephen at Macduff in 1932 was the seventeenth fishing boat to have a Kelvin diesel engine.

Introduced earlier that year the Kelvin diesel was designed to work reliably in the hands of fishermen

George Bergius, son of Kelvin's founder Walter Bergius, told me GALILEE had the tenth Model K2 two cylinder 44hp 750rpm to be produced.

Sam Winspear, who fished aboard GALILEE, said "When new she had the only Kelvin diesel engine on the English east coast. It was started by hand and had gear and throttle control in the wheelhouse".

Built in six weeks GALILEE measured 44ft with 14ft beam and was one of twenty-five boats produced by Stephen in 1932.

GALILEE WY68 was built at Macduff in 1932. Note her rudder, furled mizzen sail and galley chimney.

The majority of these were for Scottish fishermen who were replacing their steam driven herring drifters with these cost-saving motor boats and Stephen had as many as seven on the stocks at a time.

Manoeuvrable

Between 1930 and the late 1990s more than fifty Scottish-built boats have belonged to Whitby, the fishermen obtaining replacements as design has advanced and fishing methods changed.

ENDEAVOUR WY1, built in 1934 by Reekie at Anstruther was among the first canoe sterned boats to arrive.

Measuring 46ft with 14ft 6in beam she had a three cylinder 52hp Ruston and Hornsby diesel engine, a belt driven capstan and an auxiliary ketch rig. Fishing vessels were still required by the insurance companies to carry a certain amount of sail in case of emergency.

The herring ring netter FALCON, built by James N Miller and Sons at St Monans in 1921, had introduced the canoe stern to Scotland. A ring net was used to encircle a shoal of herring and was worked by two boats.

Ring netters needed to be light and manoeuvrable and fast with a quick and easy turn, so they had shallow draught and rounded forefoot.

ENDEAVOUR WY1 constructed in 1934 was one of the first canoe sterned Scottish-built boats to join the Whitby fleet.

The buoyant canoe stern with rudder tucked underneath dispensed with the projecting fifie sternpost and rudder which had caused resistance when the boats were turning and was easily damaged or entangled with fishing gear.

There was a colossal herring fishery in the 1940s and '50s as the shoals had built up during World War 2, and markets were recovering.

Over a hundred Scottish ringers and drifters were based at Whitby during the Yorkshire herring season from July until October and the local keelboats took part.

The two fishing methods had advantages and drawbacks. In rough weather and strong tides it was difficult to operate ring nets and transfer crews from one boat to the other.

Drifters preferred a full moon and could fish in worse weather and spring tides.

Although the Whitby men did some ring netting they thought herring caught by drift net was of superior quality because it was not mixed up with a mess of spawn and scales.

Drift nets were hung vertically like a curtain in the path of the herring shoals.

ENDEAVOUR's last skipper was Matt Hutchinson who joined his father, Matt Snr, in 1959. He described a typical fishing year.

"We were at the herring drifting until September. We had twenty to twenty-five nets whereas the big Scottish boats had a hundred or so".

"Then we worked pots and lines until Christmas. My mother and auntie baited the lines with mussels".

"After Christmas we went potting till May or June and then had a re-paint".

"Then we did overing, using lines with big hooks for turbot, baiting the hooks aboard the boat with herring or mackerel".

ENDEAVOUR got a Kelvin 88hp K4 diesel engine in the 1940s and an echosounder in 1962.

Like EASTER MORN, ENDEAVOUR was also filmed. A surrealist sketch on the TV show 'It's a Square

World' showed men aboard her playing whist, but using fish in place of cards!

Fuller bodied

But things were changing for the keelboats. Line fishing became uneconomical owing to the high cost of mussels, lines and hooks as well as labour for baiting. High bait prices also made crabbing unprofitable, and also the herring shoals were diminishing.

Echosounders and position finders made it possible to hunt and find fish more actively.

Some skippers acquired larger powerful fuller-bodied cruiser sterned boats with greater deck space and bigger wheelhouses, for Scottish flydragging seining and inshore trawling for white fish.

In 1960 Skipper James Leadley had SUCCESS KY211 built at Anstruther by Smith and Hutton (Shipbuilders) Ltd. Measuring 55ft x 17ft she was a characteristic small sturdy Scottish seine netter with fully developed cruiser stern.

A study in shapes in the Dock End in Whitby during the early 1960s. The Scottish-built seiner trawler SUCCESS KY211 had pretty and subtle lines. BAY WYKE WY10 was a hefty Danish type anchor seiner constructed by Whitby Boatbuilding and Repairing Co with heavy cruiser stern.

Seine net fishing with SUCCESS KY211. The cod end full of fish is being hoisted aboard. Note the coil of rope in the foreground.

She had lovely subtle lines. Skipper Leadley said she was an excellent seaboat and told me "She takes some punishment. She's very good at running before a heavy following sea because she is not too full aft".

Her fittings included Gardner 114hp diesel engine, seine net winch and rope coiler, radiotelephone, echosounder and a Decca Navigator.

During her first year she used thirty-five to forty drift nets during the herring season. From November to January she worked six longlines and 450 crab pots. In 1961 she turned to fly dragging seining full time.

Flydragging seine netting for bottom-swimming fish such as cod, haddock and flatfish, used a funnel shaped net attached to the winch by long ropes.

As the boat moved ahead she hauled the ropes which converged and herded the fish into the path of the net which was finally lifted aboard..

Net design, rope length and hauling speed varied according to weather and tide conditions, water depth, the type of seabed and the species of fish being sought.

In the terrible winter of 1962-3 SUCCESS went to Bridlington during a storm to be equipped for trawling. A trawl winch was fitted forward of the wheelhouse and the seine winch was retained for seine netting in the summer.

Trawling was more productive in dark weather and could be done over rocky ground further inshore. The seabed off Whitby has many peaks and troughs. Wire warps were used and otter boards kept the net open.

Nets were shorter than seine nets and tighter in the belly or underside, to prevent them snagging on rocks.

In 1964 SUCCESS was fitted with Decca D202 radar. After 1963 there was a big increase in the use of radar by smaller fishing craft, for position fixing in relation to shore and buoys, and safe manoeuvring in poor visibility.

Stalwart

Scotland's oldest boatyard James N Miller and Sons, founded in 1747, built several stalwart cruiser sterned seiners for Whitby, featuring the 'Queen Mary bow'.

The forward-raking straight stem presented less resistance to the water, enabling the seiner to be speedier and cover more ground with each haul of her net.

PROVIDER KY201 built by James N Miller and Sons had the 'Queen Mary bow' and a full afterbody.

The bluffer flared bow afforded more deckroom for safer operation of winch and ropes, and threw the water aside instead of over the fishermen, and the stem itself was of new construction with the aft siding greater than that at the face.

A fuller heavier afterbody gave more cabin and deck space aft and held the boat steadier in rough weather.

PROVIDER KY201 built in 1958 for Skipper John James Storr was 55ft long with 17ft beam and a Gardner 152hp engine. She had these features.

WAKEFUL KY261 delivered in 1960 to Skipper George Storr was similar, but shorter at 50ft long and powered by a Gardner engine of 114hp.

Affectionately known as 'Wakey' she fished from Whitby until being carved into pieces under the infamous fishing boat decommissioning programme. I was in the little group of miserable people watching her being cut up on the floating dock in the dismal half-light of a January morning in 1996.

One onlooker remarked "Poor old lass!".

During her later years WAKEFUL worked as a trawler.

Heftier

Since the mid 1960s Whitby keelboats have developed an increasingly important trawl fishery. Cod in particular tend to congregate around rocks and obstacles such as wrecks.

The development was hastened by the use of hard wearing synthetic twines.

Boats became even heftier and more powerful in order to pull increasingly robust gear over even rougher ground.

The trawler VENUS FR79 caused a stir on arrival in 1971. Fuller and beamier she had a transom stern which afforded more space aft on deck and below.

Built by James Noble (Fraserburgh) Ltd she measured 54ft with 18ft beam and had a Gardner 230 hp engine. Skipper Jacob Cole had a good knowledge of the inshore trawling grounds and one stretch of seabed was known as 'Jake's Garden'.

Noble had already built ten or so buxom cruiser sterned trawlers for the Yorkshire ports of Scarborough and Bridlington and was perhaps the only Scottish yard to build a traditional English square sterned coble, the 29ft x 9ft ANGELA MAY, delivered to Filey in 1962.

In 1972 Mackay Boatbuilders at Arbroath built the 55ft by 18ft cruiser sterned trawler PROVIDER AH71 for Skipper James Storr. Having full lines for her time, she carried her beam well forward to give good deck space and fish carrying capability, and counteract the weight of Gardner 230hp engine and hydraulic winch pump.

Hydraulic power enabled the winch hauling speed to be infinitely variable, from inching to maximum.

The 56ft 6in long and 18ft 3in beam transom sterned SCORESBY WY235, built by Noble in 1978 for Skipper Tal Bennison was a somewhat larger fuller version of VENUS but much more powerful so as to handle heavier gear in deeper water on rougher ground.

The transom sterned VENUS FR79 arriving in Whitby after her delivery trip from James Noble (Fraserburgh) Ltd.

Her Kelvin 375hp engine running at 1200rpm drove through a 3$\frac{1}{2}$:1 reduction gearbox to the 58in diameter propeller housed in a Kort nozzle.

A cylindrical ring of aeorofoil section steel fitted around the propeller, the nozzle gave an increase in pulling power when the trawl was being towed.

SCORESBY also had sonar, for looking around at seabed obstructions, and a fishroom chilling plant to keep catches in top condition

Existing boats took advantage of re-engining grants to get more horsepower and work heavier gear.

VENUS was given a Volvo 365hp motor with 5:1 reduction gear and 55in propeller in a Kort nozzle.

Big gear reductions and large diameter slower turning propellers with shallow pitch can also improve thrust and allow heavier trawls to be towed.

In the 1990s VENUS was fitted with a five-bladed propeller to give even better towing capabilities and reduce vibration.

JASPER 11 PD174 had much fuller lines than was formerly possible in boats designed for fishermen who did not hold a skipper's certificate. The shelterdeck was a later addition.

Profound effect

One Noble trawler, built in 1981 for Peterhead and later sold to Whitby, had two claims to fame. JASPER II PD174 was the final boat built at the yard, which had produced some 360 vessels since its founding in 1932.

She was also the first in Scotland designed and built in compliance with new regulations which had a profound effect on the subsequent development of the under 60ft (18.28m) class of boat.

The Merchant Shipping (United Kingdom, Fishing Vessels; Manning) Regulation 1980 stipulated that boats below 16.5m Registered Length need not have a certificated skipper. The rule formerly applied to boats with a Scottish Part IV Registry of under 25 Gross Tons.

Because this was a measurement of volume, those under 25 Tons were restricted in beam and depth in proportion to length.

Registered Length is measured from fore side of rudder stock to face of stem so the new regulations enabled boats less than 16.5m to be beamier, deeper and fuller than under the 25 Ton rule.

They could encompass almost double the volume with beneficial effects on stability and endurance and fishing capabilities, and were able to carry more top weight such as powerful hauling equipment, steel or aluminium shelterdecks, and spacious living and working areas.

With overall length of 59ft, Registered Length of 53.5ft (just short of 16.5m), beam of 21.5ft and depth of 12.4ft JASPER II had Part IV Tonnage of 49.83.

Skipper Richard Brewer said "She had as much below the water as above, with full bilges running the whole length of her".

"She drew 12ft which for a sixty-footer is a lot. She was a hell of a safe boat and swung a huge monster of a 72in diameter propeller. She was re-engined in 1986 with a 415hp Kelvin".

Richard said that Noble boats were renowned for towing efficiency. "They're full bellied with deep bilges and have a lot of boat round the after end with a wide transom stern" he told me. "They have a lot more propeller aperture so they can have big propellers for trawling".

Whitby keelboats were mainly 60ft overall length or less, which under a local byelaw allowed them to trawl within three miles of certain sections of coastline.

Rockhoppers

Traditionally they did side trawling whereby both warps passed to the winch over blocks hung from U-shaped gallows at starboard bow and quarter.

In the 1980s rockhopper gear was evolved. Incorporating rubber discs, known as pancakes, along the ground rope at the leading lower edge of the net it bounces over obstacles with snagging less likely.

Arnold Locker, whose firm Locker Trawlers owned several keelboats, told me "There is a good cod fishery within three miles. There is a lot of twisting and turning around fasteners and obstacles. Side trawling is easier when freeing caught nets, and the gear can be laid along the starboard deck area for mending".

"The use of GPS navigators and sonar and video plotters enables us to work closer to wrecks".

Arnold stressed that the fishermen were conservation conscious.

Although the legal minimum mesh size for cod-ends was 100mm the skippers were staunch supporters of the 110mm mesh which caught fewer undersize fish.

During the mid 1990s the keelboats worked a greater variety of fishing areas.

The Graveyard Ground, forty miles NNE of Whitby, was a good area for cod and haddock among numerous wartime wrecks.

The Licence and Brandy Grounds were very rocky patches close inshore nearer home and where the boats got a lot of lobsters in the nets.

In summer several boats worked up to 280 miles away on the oilfields off Scotland.

Arnold Locker said "The oil installations have altered the North Sea habitat. A lot of cod, ling and coley are collecting along the pipelines".

SOPHIE

The transom sterned SOPHIE LOUISE WY168, built by Miller in 1988, was Whitby's first newly built large steel trawler. Steel had several advantages for fishing boat construction including strength, and resistance to hard knocks from heavy trawl gear.

Since the early 1970s there had been a tremendous switch to all-welded steel hulls in the below 80ft section of the British fishing fleet.

Measuring 59.9ft overall with beam of 22ft SOPHIE LOUISE was a new chunky full bodied under-16.5m Registered Length design from Miller with layout arranged to meet Whitby requirements.

Her enclosed shelterdeck extended to the port gunwhale, leaving the starboard deck area open for side trawling on snaggy ground. But stern trawling was preferable for longer tows with the massive 'scraper' trawl over smooth ground in deep water at the Devil's Hole some 150 miles NE of Whitby.

Scrapers were wide shallow nets designed to catch valuable species such as monkfish which lie buried in sand.

Warps were towed from gallows at port and starboard quarters and the scraper net was hauled around a hydraulic net drum aft as it was too big to be handled on the starboard deck area.

SOPHIE's Kelvin 495hp and 1315rpm engine drove through a 4:1 reduction gearbox to a 67in propeller in a Kort nozzle.

One of her echosounders received signals from a transducer fitted on the fishing gear.

This helped to avoid fouling the net on pipelines when working rockhopper trawls on the oilfields.

Splendid

In 1995 Locker Trawlers bought a splendid keelboat from Peterhead owners. Ideal for Whitby needs

REBECCA WY477 built as HEADWAY IV PD229 in 1990 sets out for a trawling trip shortly after joining the Whitby keelboat fleet in1995. Note her full width shelterdeck.

Arnold Locker said "She has the reputation for being a very good towing boat. These Scottish boats suit us down to the ground".

REBECCA's full width shelterdeck provided more comfortable working conditions but permitted stern trawling only.

Rockhopper or scraper nets were worked from net drums at the stern.

Arnold said "After thirty years of side-winding (side trawling) we are now getting used to stern trawling".

A big shift

There was a big shift in 1997 towards even larger well chosen second-hand keelboats able to fish even further afield and target unconventional species.

By now, more skippers had the necessary qualifications to enable them to have boats above 16.5m Registered Length.

Against changing political and economic circumstances Whitby fishermen were determined to make a go of things and adapt their experiences and skills to develop new fisheries and take advantage of changing marketing opportunities.

Bigger boats enabled them to go 200 to 350 miles north of Whitby for non-quota ling, monkfish catfish, pollack, torsk and redfish, thereby spreading the variety of fish being sold on Whitby fishmarket.

Salesmen began to find new outlets for these species, particularly in Europe. Redfish for instance were popular in France.

Locker Trawlers bought the wooden hulled transom sterned 75ft by 21.8ft COROMANDEL KY27 and the 67ft by 21.3ft ARIANE LK52 built respectively by James N Miller and Sons and J and G Forbes and Co in 1984.

They represented the stage reached in the evolution of Scottish-built vessels in the 1980s with deep and full hull forms.

Both had variable pitch propellers. Blade pitch

and capable of strenuous fishing the wooden hulled transom sterned HEADWAY IV PD229, renamed REBECCA WY477, was 54ft 10in long with 21ft 2in beam and Scottish Part IV Tonnage of 38.36.

She was short enough to work inshore legally but her seaworthiness and fuel and catch carrying capacities allowed her to make longer trips to the oilfields.

Built by Gerrard Brothers at Arbroath in 1990 she was portly and full bodied with deep bilges and aft sections and high freeboard. She had Caterpillar 380 hp and 1800rpm engine with 6:1 reduction gear and 64in propeller.

could be adjusted to give maximum pull for trawling and good free running speed for going the longer distances.

Twin rigging

Skippers were also looking at twin rig trawling whereby two nets were towed side by side and usually three towing warps were used.

Twin-riggers could improve their catch rates without having to make longer trips and could thereby land fresher fish.

Hugely successful in Scotland the method had higher fishing capabilities by having the bellies of two nets rather than one in contact with the seabed and yet the spread of the gear was not much more than that with a single net.

Skipper Richard Brewer bought the 74ft x 21ft 10in RESPLENDENT PD298 built by J and G Forbes as the seiner trawler FAIR MORN INS308 in 1981. The wooden hulled transom sterned boat was among the first to have a three-quarter-length shelterdeck at the time of her building.

Richard renamed her ARRIVAIN III WY170 and

had her fitted for twin rig trawling with a three-drum winch and also a gantry carrying three towing blocks.

Lengthened

One or two skippers tried different things.

Skipper Howard Locker with SOPHIE LOUISE sometimes landed in Grimsby with red mullet caught off the Dutch coast. This non-quota species fetches high prices.

Late in 1997 SOPHIE was taken to Coastal Marine Boatbuilders Ltd at Eyemouth where she was lengthened to 73ft and converted into a stern trawler with a full length shelterdeck spanning her full width.

She was cut in two between engineroom and fishroom and a new 13ft 6in prefabricated section inserted and welded into place.

Her existing two drum North Sea Winches trawl winch was moved from the port side to a centreline position to permit stern trawling.

For safety the warps were led over the shelter top to the towing gantry thereby keeping them away from the catch handling area on main deck.

Two new North Sea Winches net drums were positioned aft and nets were worked through transom hatches. Additional tanks increased the fuel capacity from 14,000 litres to 20,000 litres and the longer fishroom doubled the catch carrying capacity from 400 to 800 boxes.

Other improvements included new power block and crane and fish reception hopper, and new lavatory and shower facilities.

Macduff Ship Design handled the design work and stability calculations for the conversion.

Howard told me "The alterations will give more safety and comfort for working further afield. We want a bit of a decent ship to go there in bad weather"

Left: ARRIVAN III WY170 built by J and G Forbes and Co at Sandhaven is equipped for twin rig trawling. She was originally the seiner trawler FAIR MORN INS308.

SOME GRP BOATS

Widely accepted

By the 1970s GRP, or glass reinforced plastics, had become a widely accepted material for building fishing boat hulls.

Although in some parts of the world vessels of 80ft long and even bigger were being moulded in GRP the market for boats under 50ft was showing the most significant growth.

GRP is basically laminated sheets or mats of synthetic fibres known as glass, which are saturated with a polyester resin.

It is easily formed and pliable and when the resin has set the resulting product is strong and hard with good resistance to water absorption.

The sheets of fibres have various characteristics.

Chopped strand mat for example consists of fibres compressed together whereas woven rovings are akin to cloth and help create a strong laminate.

For many years GEORGE WEATHERILL K24 was the largest GRP fishing boat in Great Britain.

Typically a GRP hull is built up from an outer shiny coloured gel coat and layers of resin and chopped strand mat and woven rovings and an inner coating of resin.

The GRP hull is formed or 'laid up' inside a mould which conforms to the shape of the boat being built. Moulding must be done in correct humidity and temperature conditions and the specialist firms who produce GRP hulls exercise vigorous quality control to ensure that defects are not formed during the laminating process.

Many firms produce the hulls to be fitted out by other boatbuilders and individuals.

Boats built of GRP generally require less maintenance than a wooden or steel hull of similar type.

Numerous small English square sterned cobles and some double-enders have been built in the material with the laminate shaped to look like clinker planking.

For many years the 54ft Whitby transom sterned seiner trawler GEORGE WEATHERILL K24 was the UK's largest GRP fishing vessel.

Designed by Scottish naval architects G L Watson and Co, she was built in 1973 to the order of businessman Teddy Jarman and initially skippered by Ian Britton.

Teddy Jarman said "I just had a feeling that GRP should be tried for a fishing boat. I had an instinctive feeling that it was the right stuff".

GEORGE WEATHERILL's hull including GRP deck, deckhouse and whaleback was moulded by Halmatic (Scotland) Ltd in the Orkney Islands and she was fitted out in Middlesbrough by E and L B Pinkney Marine.

Sadly she was decommissioned and broken up in the late 1990s.

Favoured increasingly

GRP became favoured increasingly for smaller vessels in many ports.

The SFIA 1993 report on boatbuilding shows that

some 1,848 new GRP boats under 10m joined the UK fishing vessel register between 1981 and 1990 compared with 294 steel and 330 wooden hulled ones.

During the same decade only 100 or so boats of 10m and above were built of GRP while around 253 were steel and 186 of timber construction.

The preference for small GRP boats continued into the 1990s, some 150 below 10m being built in 1992 as against 16 in steel and 27 in wood.

Numerous GRP boats joined Whitby's mini keelboat fleet.

Fitted out

In 1996 Skipper Harry Hoggarth started potting with his new below 10m GRP boat DEEP HARMONY IV WY478.

She was based on a K26 hull from Kingfisher Boats of Falmouth in Cornwall and was fitted out in Whitby by Steve Cook.

With broad transom stern, round bilges and raked stem and a working deck area of 17 sq m the K26 measured 8m overall with 3.40m beam and 1.20m draught.

Kingfisher supplied her complete with GRP wheelhouse and whaleback.

Forward, the hull had a French-style flare to the lower and mid bow quarters but a knuckle in the upper section enabled the premoulded whaleback to be fitted.

Harry chose the Kingfisher hull because she was robust and roomy for her size.

He said "Steve has done a marvellous job fitting her out. Every bolt used in her is stainless steel. Even the rudder is stainless steel".

DEEP HARMONY IV WY478 was fitted out in Whitby. Her GRP hull with wheelhouse and whaleback came from Kingfisher Boats in Cornwall.

95

At Whitby she was fitted with wooden deck beams spaced at 16in or so, and the deck was constructed from marine plywood and four coats of GRP and surfaced with a non slip gel coat.

Two watertight marine plywood bulkheads faced with GRP were glassed in forward of and abaft the engine.

Oak gunwhales capped with aluminium strips, and a plastic outer gunwhale were added, and stainless steel mooring cleats positioned at the quarters and on the whaleback.

An oak rubbing strip was fitted from stern to shoulders, and the wheelhouse, which was offset to port, was lined in marine plywood with mahogany trim and a wooden door fitted.

A secondary steering and engine control console was placed outside the wheelhouse near the fishing gear hauling position.

Much of DEEP HARMONY IV's equipment including Ford 120hp diesel engine, Spencer Carter pot hauler, Furuno colour echosounder and Wills Ridley steering gear was transferred from Harry's previous mini keelboat DEEP HARMONY III which had been decommissioned.

Harry worked crab and lobster pots and longlines. He said he disliked gill and trammel nets because it could be dangerous should he need to go to sea and retrieve them in worsening weather.

By early 1998 more than sixty K26 boats had been supplied to UK skippers including another for Whitby.

Named NAZANNA WY780 this was fitted out early that year by Skipper Adrian Roe as replacement to a decommissioned coble.

Adrian chose the K26 as she provided a lot of beam for her length and, unlike the coble, would enable him to work pots and nets at the same time.

COBLES FROM NORTHUMBERLAND

Exchange of ideas

Some Yorkshire fishermen had cobles built elsewhere.

J & J Harrison Ltd at Amble in Northumberland produced several for Whitby starting with the 32ft ENTERPRISE 11 WY47 for Skipper Wilf Allen in 1946.

She was followed by RESOLUTION WY7, WHITBY LASS WY3 and SILVER LINE WY108.

The 30ft CORONATION QUEEN WY75 was delivered to Skipper William Harrison of Staithes in 1953 and the 31ft SEA LOVER WY99 to Skipper George Hanson also of Staithes, in 1954.

Both these cobles were powered by Kelvin Ricardo 15hp petrol engines and were supplied with auxiliary cotton dipping lug sails.

All these cobles were half-decked and the propeller was housed in a box tunnel formed over a cut-away area in the bottom planking between the drafts.

Harrison's master boatbuilder Hector Handyside told me that the 31ft x 8ft 8in half-decked coble STAR OF HOPE WY223 built for Staithes skipper Matt Verril in 1965 was the first Harrison coble to have a Whitby-style raised ram tunnel, made by bending the bottom planking into a concavity.

Matt had been part owner of GOLDEN CROWN WY78 built by William Clarkson in 1953 and was happy with the efficiency of her raised ram tunnel.

STAR OF HOPE was powered by a Petter three cylinder 33.75hp water cooled diesel engine and carried hydraulic pot hauler and Ferrograph echosounder.

First wheelhouse

Harrison's first coble with a wheelhouse was GUIDE ME WY161 built for Whitby fishermen Bob and John Walker in 1960. At 38ft 6in x 11ft and powered by a Gardner 3LW 48hp engine she was at that time the yard's biggest coble.

She had greater beam than usual and higher freeboard with twelve planks rather than eleven to carry the extra weight of the larger engine and give better stability to bear the topweight produced by the wheelhouse.

Fitted abaft the half-deck the wheelhouse had Columbian pine tongue and groove planks on a redwood frame and was lined with marine plywood.

A special system of mechanical steering was devised with chains leading aft in pipes along either side below the gunwhale and attached to a special tiller which could be removed for unshipping the rudder.

GUIDE ME had a mechanically driven pot hauler from the Brit Engineering Co and carried Woodsons radio and Ferrograph echosounder.

A small formica lined cabin was arranged below the half deck.

Harrison cobles were celebrated for their sleek and trim and elegant lines and high standards of craftsmanship. Founded in 1870 the firm built more than three hundred cobles the majority for Northumberland owners. Generally speaking many Northumberland fishermen preferred a lower longer-bodied finer lined more rakish coble to the often chunkier Yorkshire ones.

GUIDE ME WY161 built in 1960 was the first coble from J & J Harrison Ltd at Amble to have a wheelhouse.

7. WHITEHALL SHIPYARD

Moonlight and phosphorescence

Although cobles and double-enders were my early enthusiasms a trip to the herring grounds with the 52ft cruiser sterned keelboat LEAD US II A291 aroused my interest in other types of Whitby-built boats.

The trip was full of delightful sights, with moonlight and green phosphorescence and everyone covered in thousands of opalescent herring scales which filled the air as the fishermen shook the fish out of the nets and onto deck.

Later there was thick fog and a cacophony of honks and whistles and booms and wheezes from dozens of nearby herring drifters and ring-netters.

LEAD US II was built for Skipper Raymond Storr in 1959 by the Whitby Shipbuilding and Engineering Company, earlier known as Whitby Boatbuilding and Repairing Co.

Between World War 2 and the 1980s this yard had various names and a sometimes troubled life. Several times it went into receivership and passed to new owners.

It was started in a small way on the west bank of the Esk by local businessmen during the 1939-45 War and built lifeboats as part of the war effort.

Then the firm moved across river and in 1947 launched the 60ft x 17ft 6in anchor seiner PETRENDA for Grimsby owners. The yard had tendered for this type of vessel, known as scrobs or scrogs in Whitby and snibbies in Grimsby, because they were in keen demand among English owners and ex-patriot Danes particularly in Grimsby.

The seine net was originated in Denmark by Jens Laursen Vaever in the nineteenth century and was initially used for catching plaice. By 1918 the North Sea was super-abundant in fish after low catching activity during World War 1 and Danish anchor seiners landed massive catches at English ports.

Many Danish fishermen settled in Britain largely in the Grimsby area in the inter-war years and later.

Particularly suited to plaice and cod capture, Danish anchor seining was done on large areas of smooth and sandy seabed. The funnel shaped net had two long warps, one attached to either side of the mouth.

The anchor was dropped overboard and the end of the first warp attached to the anchor buoys. Then the boat motored away in a semicircle, paying out warp.

After setting the net with its mouth facing into the oncoming tide, she completed a circle back to the anchor buoys with the second warp.

She lay at anchor and hauled the warps which converged and herded the fish into the path of the net.

Seagoing dumplings

By 1960 about a hundred anchor seiners were registered in Grimsby with about half of them built in British yards. Typical Danish anchor seiners were exceptionally stalwart and able to cope with fiendish weather. A Danish skipper visited Whitby Boatbuilding and gave advice on PETRENDA's design.

PETRENDA was followed by WHITEHAVEN for Grimsby and BAY WYKE WY10, VAN WYKE WY30 and EVE'S WY44 for Whitby companies.

Derivative of Danish hull forms and layout these five were the most amazing shapes and have been described as 'sea-going dumplings'.

They were deep draughted to grip the water and maintain position when hauling gear broadsides on. They had full lines with tremendously full cruiser stern and immense buttocks all in the interests of seakeeping and catch carrying capabilities.

The cruiser stern in which the sides terminate at the centre line and the fullest part is at or below the waterline, gives support in the water.

A full bodied boat with cruiser stern is not easily overwhelmed from behind and turned sideways by following seas. Anchor seiners needed the ability to ride the sea at anchor.

Construction was massive with 2½ in planks and double oak frames and they carried sufficient fuel for three-week trips and could carry twenty tons of fish.

They had auxiliary ketch rig with foresail, mainsail and mizzen to help hold them steady when hauling gear.

All about EVE'S

All but EVE'S had three-cylinder 120hp Lister diesel engines.

Built in 1951 EVE'S was powered by an air-starting Swedish June-Munktell 120hp and 325rpm two stroke two-cylinder hot bulb engine turning the 57in controllable pitch propeller by direct drive.

Low revving hot bulb engines were often fitted to fishing boats particularly in Scandinavia as they were dependable and durable and simple to operate and economical on fuel.

EVE'S WY44, one of the 'seagoing dumplings', with full heavy cruiser stern.

The combustion chamber, often called the hot bulb, was positioned above the cylinder and linked to it by a narrow passage. Oil was injected into the chamber and ignited by the combined influences of the compression and the heat of the combustion chamber walls.

The hot bulb was heated to a dull red heat by a blowlamp before the engine was started.

Hot bulb engines were somewhat large and heavy for their power output.

Whitby people remember EVE'S for the slow 'pom pom' sound of her engine. The exhaust vapours emerged as perfect smoke-rings from the exhaust pipe alongside the wheelhouse.

EVE'S was built for anchor seining but was also equipped for line fishing off the Faeroe Islands and Iceland.

She carried 1,700 gallons of fuel. The engine provided belt drive for the Grumsen seine net winch and for the hydraulic pump which powered the line hauler abaft the maimast. A Stuart Turner auxiliary motor charged the lighting batteries and drove the compressor which filled the air bottles for main engine starting.

Wheelhouse fittings included Marconi radiotelephone and echosounder.

EVE'S had the reputation of holding her position well when hauling seine nets, owing to her deep draught.

EVE'S fished from Whitby for two or three years round about 1960.

Her first landing there was 340 stones, mainly cod.

Whitby fisherman Colin Kipling was a crew-member at that time. He said "With a crew of four we did 21-day trips anchor seining on smooth ground in the North Sea, fishing twenty hours a day. Fish was stowed in ice on shelves".

Between the whiles, the yard looked to smaller things. One of these was my father's 19ft double-ender MERINA WY19 built in 1947 and used for part time fishing with a dozen lobster pots and some hand lines.

I remember trips on green choppy seas amid clouds of spray.

In the early post-war years Whitby Boatbuilding also produced large carvel planked double-enders known as 'mules' for Scarborough.

A typical example was 33ft long with 9ft 6in beam, powered by a 26-30hp Kelvin Ricardo petrol engine and planked with larch on 2in x 4in grown oak frames at 1ft intervals.

She set a mizzen steadying sail, offset slightly to port to leave space aft for a Hyland pot hauler.

Some mules were larger at 37ft with 33hp Kelvin diesel engines.

Classic ring netter

Unlike many fishing boat builders, which concentrated on the development of one particular class of vessel within a limited size range, Whitby Boatbuilding produced a variety.

LEAD US WY36 was akin to a classic Scottish herring ring netter.

LEAD US WY36 built for Skipper William Storr in 1950 was similar to a classic Scottish ring netter.

This method had been developed by the Scots for catching herring swimming in tight shoals in relatively sheltered waters. Two boats were used.

Ring netters needed to be nimble and manoeuvrable and speedy with a quick, tight and easy turn, yet sea-kindly and able to carry huge catches.

They had shallow draught and rounded forefoot, an easy entry and clean run aft yet had firm bilges to prevent excessive rolling and give good carrying space.

The propeller aperture and rudder were tucked well underneath the buoyant canoe stern to avoid entanglement with the net. Freeboard and bulwarks were shallow for ease of working the gear and a slight flare forward threw the water aside.

The wheelhouse was small to conserve deck space. Ring netters were admired for their sweet and elegant lines.

Measuring 50ft x 16ft LEAD US had a Kelvin 88hp diesel engine.

At various times she worked pots, lines, herring drift nets and ring nets. WHITBY ROSE WY110 built in 1957 for Skipper Alf Locker was a similar vessel.

ACCORD WY130 ashore at Whitby.

ACCORD WY130 and STAKESBY ROSE WY120 completed in 1958 for Whitby skippers William Graham and Jack Locker had similar dimensions to LEAD US but were deeper with stronger sheer and built with flydragging seining in mind.

Flydragging seiners could work on limited patches of smooth ground and thereby make shorter trips nearer to Whitby.

Wine glass shaped

Around this time the yard was renamed Whitby Shipbuilding and Engineering Company.

Between 1954 and 1962 the firm built some eleven anchor seiners, the majority for Grimsby and all of finer hull form than the suet-pudding-like EVE'S and sister ships and starting with the 56ft x 16ft BEKIMA GY182 in 1955.

The others included BELLONA GY326, KEVAN GY502, WARDLEY GY416, WALDRIAN GY474, WALPAUL GY589, LYNMAY GY633, MAW WYKE WY153, EJLENA GY627, SANDWYKE WY167 and IRIS DEAN GY701.

Anchor-seine netter SANDWYKE WY167 under construction. She had closely spaced double frames.

Hugh Gollogly, who did the lofting work for BEKIMA when he was only nineteen, told me "EVE'S was a bulky boat with big radius stern. BEKIMA was more wine glass shaped in section and her floors were more hollow with more deadrise and bilges not so full".

"She had finer forward lines with leaner entry. Her sharper stern had more tumblehome and together with finer quarters and run made her sit at anchor like a bird on a nest and let the water flow past".

On the bevel

Yard manager and draughtsman Marcus Fletcher devised a detailed and precise measurement procedure at the lofting stage to produce extremely accurate templates for BEKIMA's frames and to calculate the required degrees of bevel.

This enabled the sawmill to saw every futtock to correct shape and on the bevel rather than square. Each frame was then assembled on a jig called the 'spider' and further measured for accuracy.

As a result of this careful preparation work, minimal fairing in with the adze was required at the construction stage to get the planks to fit against the frames.

Building time was saved by 75 per cent as compared with the earlier seiners whose frames had been sawn square and needed weeks and weeks of adzing.

BEKIMA's construction was massive. Her double 3in frames which gave a 6in total siding, were spaced 15in between their centres. This left only a 9in gap between each pair of frames

Her topsides planks were 3in oak and the remainder 2in larch.

The same templates were used for the subsequent Danish seiners with two or three additional midships frames used to achieve greater length overall when needed

BEKIMA had Gardner 6L3 six cylinder 114hp

101

diesel engine with fixed pitch propeller and 3:1 reverse and reduction gearbox. There was a growing preference for electric starting faster revving lighter-weight engines.

Introduced in 1932 the L3 pleased the fishermen and remained in general use until superseded by the L3B range in 1960

BEKIMA's four speed Grumsen seine winch was driven through a dog clutch from the engine.

She carried auxiliary ketch rig with cotton foresail and mizzen, Wheelhouse fittings included Kelvin Hughes echosounder.

Happy medium

The Whitby keelboat LEAD US II A291 built in 1959 was designed to be roomy on deck and below and had strong individuality and character.

Hugh Gollogly said she was a 'one-off' with hull form a happy medium between that of EVE'S and BEKIMA in degree of fullness with good herring carrying capacity and full stern.

Above: SANDWYKE was one of the series of anchor seiners which had finer lines than those of EVE's. (Photo; author's collection).

Right: LEAD US II A291 in the Dock End in Whitby, maybe 1959 or '60. Note her cruiser stern and flared bow.

She measured 52ft x 16ft 6in beam and drew 8ft 6in of water.

There were also Scottish flydragging seiner influences in her raked straight stem and bluff flared bow which afforded more deckroom for the coils of rope and safer operation of the winch.

She had Gardner 6L3 114hp engine, and her Fifer many purpose winch, made in Scotland by boatbuilders James N Miller and Sons, enabled her to work a variety of fishing methods.

Appropriate drums and barrels could be fitted to suit each activity. For example, a messenger warping drum could be fitted for hauling herring nets.

LEAD US II used a fleet of twenty nets whereas the bigger Scottish drifters fished eighty or so. At one time the drift net was the chief method of catching herring.

Sheets of netting were joined end-to-end in fleets of up to a hundred per boat, stretching for up to two miles. They hung in the water like a curtain, held vertical by floats and buoys at the top and by a weighted sole rope.

After setting the gear the drifter lay moored to the near end of the nets by a messenger rope and drifted with the elements for three or four hours. Oncoming herring were caught in the mesh by their gills.

When the fishermen hauled the nets they shook them to remove the catch.

It is this hauling procedure which I remember well from my trip with LEAD US II. Everyone disappeared in a thick storm of herring which peppered the deck like hailstones.

Plundering the stocks

During her first year LEAD US II enjoyed the last big herring fishery at Whitby. In the early 1960s huge fleets of Eastern European trawlers were thought responsible for plundering the stocks leaving insufficient space for the British boats to shoot their nets.

The overseas vessels were fishing legally as they were outside the UK three mile limit and this helped to support the call for Britain to extend her territorial waters.

One night the Whitby based fleet caught only one herring!

LEAD US II also worked flydragging seine nets, crab and lobster pots, longlines and white fish trawls. She also tried a bit of herring ring netting but proved too cumbersome for the job.

LEAD US II was one of a number of English owned boats registered at Scottish ports.

Under The Merchant Shipping Act 1894 skippers of boats measuring 25 Tons and over required a seagoing certificate. The 25 Tons was calculated in England under Part 1 of the Act, using an internal volumetric measurement based on Simpson's Rules.

In Scotland it was calculated under Part IV Registry using length, breadth and depth measurements and produced a smaller figure.

Thus a fisherman could have a somewhat roomier boat under Scottish registry without having to qualify for a 'ticket'.

The 25 Ton criterion survived until the 1980s.

Lines plan

In 1959 Whitby Shipbuilding built the 33ft Whitby coble SEA FISHER WY147. Most unusual in coble building a lines plan was drawn from which sectional moulds were made and set up 4ft apart. Hugh Gollogly, who built her, said "I put in the stern frame first and planked her to the moulds. But I did not fight it. I let the planks go where they wanted rather than forcing them up to the moulds. So I used the moulds as a guide".

Hugh used the same moulds when planking the 37ft coble JANE ELIZABETH WY144 built in 1960 but 'came off them' to create more beam.

"But building cobles from moulds was not really a great success" he said. "It was too time consuming. After this we built them by eye and from rule of thumb in the accepted way".

Liquidation

In the early 1960s Whitby Shipbuilding constructed a big new slipway to provide hauling-out facilities for repair and overhaul of fishing boats, coasters and tugs, and able to accommodate up to fourteen fishing craft, leaving one berth free for emergency use.

Sadly things went wrong. Financial difficulties forced the firm into liquidation.

Reopened as Whitehall Shipyard under new owners in 1965 it was developed into a yacht yard, marina and social centre but built some fishing boats in wood and steel.

There were several more changes of ownership during subsequent years.

Two fisheries

In 1975 Whitehall delivered the 55ft x 18ft classic Scottish type wooden hulled transom sterned seiner trawler SUCCESS LH81 to Skipper James Leadley. By the early 1970s Whitby had fifteen seiner trawlers with only two older keelboats working pots and lines.

"Pots, lines and herring nets was a lot of gear" Jim Leadley said. "It was simpler to break things down into just two fisheries, seine and trawl".

SUCCESS was built to lines designed by Scottish naval architects G L Watson and Co. Her 230hp and 1150 rpm 8L3B Gardner engine drove through Twin Disc 3.5:1 reduction gearbox to the Bruntons fixed pitch propeller housed in a Kort nozzle.

Gardner introduced the L3B range of motors in 1960 to provide greater power more economically.

A Mastra seine and trawl winch from the Northern Tool and Gear Co at Arbroath in Scotland was fitted forward. It was powered hydraulically from a Dowty variable delivery pump from the forward end of the Gardner engine through a 2:1 step up gearbox.

As opposed to mechanical drive the pump provided infinitely variable winch speed over a wide range of engine revolutions and more flexibility in working the gear.

A Beccles seine rope coiler was driven from the winch and a Cattermarine power block was fitted abaft the deckhouse. Consisting of a hydraulically powered rotating sheave on a derrick the power block came into use in the UK seiner trawler fleet in the 1960s. Seine nets were hauled through the block as far as the cod-end which was then lifted on board by the gilson derrick.

Use of the block made net hauling safer and less arduous and enabled gear to be worked in worse weather and heavier catches handled.

Configuration of the gear handling equipment on SUCCESS met Jim Leadley's particular requirements and enabled her to go to sea equipped to work trawls or seines as required.

The arrangement for hauling seine ropes was unusual. The starboard ropes travelled from the coiler down into a storage bin below deck.

This left room for gutting fish on deck and for working side trawls. The port ropes were coiled onto deck in the normal mannner.

Rope storage bins came into use in Scotland in the 1970s but normally two were fitted, to store both sets of rope.

Much more electronic equipment was now used by this type and size of boat than a decade earlier.

SUCCESS carried Furuno FUV12 Universal Graph multi stylus echosounder, F850 sounder, and FRS24 radar, Redifon Saxon King 400W radiotelephone and GR674 vhf radiotelephone and Decca Mk21 Navigator and 450 Autopilot.

Multi stylus sounders had no moving stylus but instead had hundreds of stationary styli arranged across the paper and electronically scanned.

The multi stylus system permitted the normal depth display and a more detailed expanded scale of part of the water depth to be shown on the paper simultaneously.

Jim Leadley came ashore in 1981. He had become very active politically on behalf of British fishermen and served on various committees and became President of the National Federation of Fishermen's Organisations. In

1983 he was awarded the MBE for his services to the fishing industry.

By 1996 SUCCESS was fishing under Jim's grandson Peter Leadley but was sold away from Whitby in 1997. Along with other Whitby keelboats she had concentrated on trawling.

Seining became uneconomical because beam trawlers kept shifting the seabed obstacles and destroying the grounds.

Collapse

Meanwhile things at Whitehall Shipyard had not gone well.

On May 22 1985 all of the whole of the contents of the shipyard, two night clubs, a public house, restaurant, office block and three directors' flats were offered for sale by auction.

All manner of boatbuilding plant and paraphernalia from twenty-four rolls of caulking yarn and a half drum of pitch to an electric spindle moulding and die tapping machine (incomplete) were auctioned.

Lot Number 30 was a 31ft partially built carvel planked cruiser sterned boat. Hugh Gollogly had constructed her to near deck level using grown oak frames interspersed with steamed oak timbers.

She was bought at the auction by Lenny Oliver who later worked with boatbuilder Steve Cook. Lenny completed the 31 footer as the fishing vessel LEON with 120 hp Ford engine and forward wheelhouse.

For about a year he used her for gill and trammel netting and then sold her to owners in Tiree.

Initially designed as a motor sailer she had 11ft 6in beam and was narrow on the waterline with fine entry to go through the water well.

Built on Scottish lines the seiner trawler SUCCESS LH81 came from Whitehall Shipyard in 1975.

8. ENDINGS AND BEGINNINGS

Smashing up the fishing boats

Woeful heaps

During the mid 1990s in Whitby I saw some woeful little heaps of timber and twisted metal.

They were the remains of local cobles broken up under the European Union's decommissioning programme whereby fishermen willing to remove their boats from the fishing fleet were offered large sums of money.

During the years 1993 to 1998 inclusively, hundreds of British boats including attractive and historically important craft were taken out of commission in England, Scotland, Wales and Northern Ireland.

Many were carved up by chain saw or smashed by bulldozer, some were incinerated or buried, while others helped to make huge bonfires on November 5th.

While it was broadly realised that overfishing should be curbed and diminishing fish stocks allowed to revive, there was huge distress and protest at the policy of destroying the boats.

Robust fishermen broke down in tears at the savage destruction of these dignified vessels. One told me he had felt ill for a fortnight after seeing his family's boat made a bonfire of.

The decommissioning scheme stemmed from the EU's Multi-Annual Guidance Programme which called for a reduction in the capacity of member states' fishing fleets in terms of total tonnage and engine power.

Britain's decommissioning regulations were based on the severest suggestions under Article 8 of the EU Council Regulation No 3699/93 which stated that 'Measures to stop vessels' fishing activities may include:
- -scrapping,
- -permanent transfer to a third country,
- -permanent re-assignment of the vessel in question to uses other than fishing in Community waters.

The Ministry of Agriculture, Fisheries and Food (MAFF), which supervised the British scheme, decreed that in order to qualify for decommissioning grants the boats must be broken up or otherwise permanently disabled so that they were incapable of use for any seagoing purpose.

In 1996 a spokesman for MAFF told me "We have so far been unable to devise arrangements which would guarantee that such vessels could not at some point return to fish as part of a Member State's fleet".

Boats were required to satisfy certain conditions to be eligible for decommissioning grants.

They must be seaworthy, over ten years old at the date of the application, and over 10m overall length. They must have appropriate fishing licences, registration status and safety certificates and must have spent a specified number of days at sea in the two years preceding the grant application.

Cobles destroyed

Some lovely boats were destroyed in the Whitby area including several featured in this book.

During the winter of 1995-6 the coble ALLIANCE WY39 was cut up, her remains looking somewhat like the head and backbone of a cod.

Some relatively new cobles met their end. Late in 1996 the Scarborough based SEASPRAY J SH237 was decommissioned. She had changed hands sometime earlier, following the death of her original skipper Joseph Cooke.

Her builder Tony Goodall was upset at her destruction. "It was an act of vandalism" he said. "Joe spoke well of her".

The cobles GUIDE ME WY161, AUDREY LASS WY291, SHEILA L WY191 and SUNDRYD VIPER were also annihilated.

One or two decommissioned cobles survived but looked forlorn and lifeless.

ALLIANCE WY39 was one of the many cobles broken up under the abysmal decommissioning programme. Note her engine beds, frames and floors, and the remains of her raised ram tunnel and half deck.

MAFF told me in 1996 "We are prepared to consider proposals for donating decommissioned vessels to schools or charitable organisations."

"As a minimum, the engine, gearbox, shaft and propeller, ship's electrics and all fishing gear must be removed. The hull would also need to be made unseaworthy in some way, and this might be achieved by cutting sections out of the vessel's structure or setting it in concrete".

The Redcar coble FREEDOM WY271 was donated to a local primary school.

But boats immobilised ashore look sadly diminished and in bad taste and they deteriorate quickly.

Some absurdities were thrown up by the decommissioning programme.

Grant money could be used to purchase smaller modern more efficient boats and spare fishing licences could be bought for them.

Licences could be bought from boats which had been taken out of the fishing fleet by means other than the decommissioning programme.

A below-10m fully decked craft with wide transom stern, say, could carry more fishing gear and work in worse weather than a 33ft (10.058m) coble, and in consequence had greater catching capability than the vessel she replaced.

Boats other than cobles were put an end to. I was sad to learn that LEAD US II A291 , later renamed KRISTAND, had been done away with. In her latter years she belonged to owners in Cornwall and worked as a netter under the Plymouth registration PH345.

Touch of optimism
By the close of 1997 there was a touch of optimism, at least for boats in England and Wales.

For some time, maritime heritage organisations had been pressing for a stop to the destruction.

MAFF had approved a procedure whereby decommissioned vessels of historical interest would be owned by the National Fishing Heritage Centre in Grimsby.

They would be leased out to approved parties for restoration or preservation and allowed to be maintained as seaworthy and used for a legitimate purpose other than commercial fishing.

But the carnage continued for some.

The decommissioning of the coble HANNAH MARY WY84 resulted in yet another haphazard pile of broken planks, frames and fastenings alongside the Esk early in 1998.

A new boatbuilding yard

Engineering firm builds steel scalloper

The below-10m steel scallop dredger JACQUELINE ANNE OB555 delivered to her owners Skipper Domhnall Maclachlainn and Ian F Hall of Tobermory in 1997 was the first boat built by Parkol Marine Engineering.

Hitherto this Whitby firm had concentrated on fishing vessel repairs and modifications and engineering work.

The new boat was lifted into the water by crane from her building berth on Eskside Wharf.

Skipper Maclachlainn had earlier bought the small steel trawler SELINA ANN NN88 from Whitby and was so impressed with work done by Parkol in converting her for scalloping he decided to have JACQUELINE ANNE built by the firm.

Scallop dredging formed an important part of the fisheries of south west Scotland. Basically a dredge comprises a steel frame attached to a bag composed of linked steel rings.

Whitby's tradition of boatbuilding continues. Parkol Marine Engineering built the steel scallop dredger JACQUELINE ANNE OB555 in 1997 from components supplied in kit form. Here, her framework is being constructed.

The boat tows several dredges along the seabed, and metal teeth on the frame rake scallops into the bag.

Measuring 9.95m long overall, 4.6m beam and about 9ft draught aft JACQUELINE ANNE was of double hard chine construction whereby bottom and sides meet at two distinct angles rather than forming round bilges. It is a simple and economical method of steel boatbuilding.

The frames require no shaping into curves at the bilges and the plates are bent into simple fore and aft curves rather than into complex double ones.

JACQUELINE ANNE's forefoot bulged forward to form a semi bulbous bow which can increase directional stability and give a longer waterline length.

Stability

In the interests of high stability characteristics she was exceptionally chunky and deep and beamy. Legislation regarding stability standards was introduced for boats measuring 12m Registered Length or over as part of The Fishing Vessel (Safety Provisions) Rules 1975. It would also form an essential part of the Marine Safety Agency's proposed new under-12m code of safe practice which was at a consultation stage in 1997.

JACQUELINE ANNE was designed by Ian Paton MRINA from Scottish naval architects S C McAllister and Company.

In fact she complied with the existing 12m and over 'Beam Trawler' stability criteria which were particularly stringent.

Ian Paton told me "She is designed to be as big a boat as possible with an under 10m licence, yet perform a demanding role, hence her stumpy appearance. Beam had to be high for stability. This was essential. However, a waterline length to beam ratio of 2:1 is not really ideal for steering, so to give improved directional stability we chose to have a deep keel and put the rudder as far aft as possible".

Skipper Maclachlainn said "Our criterion is to go to sea in a safe boat for ourselves and our crew. The general trend is towards big sophisticated vessels working deep water and requiring more skills to run. We decided there was enough pressure on fish stocks so have opted for the small end of the scale. We have taken a basic and simple method of working a scalloper but with a modern hull".

JACQUELINE ANNE had bluff bow and soft nose stem, and her beam was carried well forward to enable her to work five scallop dredges each side.

To give good towing capabilities when scalloping or trawling the large diameter propeller provided greater thrust and the Kort nozzle improved the towing power.

Ian Paton said "However, for a propeller to perform well it still has to have good flow into it. If the aft buttocks are too steep the propeller will be starved of water. For this reason we opted for easy lines aft lines".

Kit form

JACQUELINE ANNE was built using a construction technique coming into greater use.

Steel-Kit Ltd of Aberystwyth took the naval architects' lines plan and steelwork drawings and used computer technology to break down the hull structure into component parts such as frames, deck and shell plating.

Centraalstaal in Holland used the Steel-Kit computer data disc to drive computer controlled underwater plasma cutting machines which cut out the components.

These components were then delivered to Parkol in kit form ready for construction. The underwater plasma cutting technique cuts the steel accurately and reduces heat distortion.

To some extent the components had notches which enabled them to interlock together thereby saving building time.

Having the plates and framework ready for fabrication eliminates the need for small yards to have costly steel forming equipment.

JACQUELINE ANNE was lifted into the water by crane. She has doubled-chine hull with semi bulbous bow and transom stern.

Generally JACQUELINE ANNE's hull was constructed from 8mm plate and was increased to 10mm in the garboard area. The double-plate rudder enhanced steering efficiency during scalloping or trawling. Her duct keel was unusual in that the sides were 15mm thick and bottom 50mm thick and 250mm wide to withstand impact should she take the ground.

Below deck JACQUELINE ANNE was subdivided from forward into engineroom, fishroom and cabin. Fuel tanks built as part of the hull structure port and starboard of the fishroom carried in total a thousand gallons.

The keel-cooled Cummins 220hp and 2,000 rpm engine turned the 4ft Teignbridge Kaplan propeller through a Twin Disc 4.5:1 reduction and reverse gearbox. The Kaplan propeller, designed for use in a nozzle, gave additional thrust and was highly resistant to impact damage.

Keel cooling means that part of the engine fresh water cooling circuit passes along pipes on the outside of the hull and is exposed to the cooling effect of seawater. It was chosen in preference to indirect heat-exchanger cooling and the problems caused by seaweed clogging up the water intakes.

From decommissioned vessels

Engine and gearbox, the winch, wheelhouse windows and the steering gear came from decommissioned fishing vessels. Domhnall said "This way we have got some good quality second hand equipment".

Two 24 volt alternators, a Jabsco bilge pump, the Jefferson Hydraulics winch pump and the compressor for the fishroom cooling plant were driven from the engine.

Attention was given to keeping scallops in good condition. The fishroom was fully insulated with a closed cell foam spray faced with marine plywood and was fitted with a small Sanden chilled air cooling plant.

In the interests of safety and to reduce deck clutter the main towing warps travelled to the towing blocks via sheaves which were boxed in inside the forward corners of the wheelhouse.

JACQUELINE ANNE also had gallows and sheaves for prawn trawling.

Electronic chart

Electronic instruments included Racal Decca Fish Master chart video plotter, two ICOM M59 radiotelephones, Cetrek 700 autopilot, and Furuno CH24 sonar, 50 kHz FCV-291 colour video echosounder, GP-80 navigator and 10in 1931 daylight-viewing radar.

The FishMaster plotter recorded and displayed successful fishing tows, fasteners and other information on an electronic chart and had route planning capabilities.

Scallops tend to live in soft ground near rocks and in dense numbers amongst solid rock, and the FCV-291 sounder provided easy evaluation of seabed conditions.

Echoes were presented on the 10in screen in up to sixteen colours. The variety of display modes included 'Bottom Discrimination' which discriminated between soft, rocky or sandy bottom by changing the colour or length of the 'tails' hanging below the seabed echo.

Electronics technology was developing continually and the GP-80 was a new GPS navigator. In the Highway Display mode one could intuitively see how to steer and where the next waypoint was located relative to the boat.

Way points were displayed on a 3D graphic image of a 'road' seen in perspective.

In 1998, Parkol, which is run by Jim Morrison and John Oliver, began building an under-16.5m Registered Length transom sterned steel trawler for Locker Trawlers.

Scheduled for completion early in 1999 she is of massive proportions with round bilges and 7m beam. She will have fine forward lines to get a good flow of water to the propeller in a Kort nozzle.

Designed by McAllister in association with her owners and constructed from a Steel-Kit 'package' she is the largest fishing boat built in Whitby since the 55-footer SUCCESS LH81 left Whitehall Shipyard in 1975.

So Whitby's tradition of boatbuilding is undergoing a significant recovery!

Whitby's fleet in the 1990s

The Whitby fleet at the start of 1998 included fifteen keelboats up to 78ft long.

A good third had sufficient horsepower and fuel and catch carrying capabilities to make economically worthwhile trips to the oil pipelines and even further afield in the North Sea.

But fishing patterns can change. For much of 1998 a prolific and lucrative codling fishery off the Yorkshire coast has helped restore Whitby to its traditional role as a predominantly inshore top quality fresh fish port.

During 1997 there had been a noticeable trend towards longer trips into Scottish waters to target non-quota species such as ling and tusk and pollack but in 1998 even the larger trawlers fished locally and landed catches every two or three days or so.

One of the newer keelboats, the below-16.5m Registered Length wooden hulled ORION II KY118 was built by Gerrard Brothers at Arbroath in 1983 for Scottish owners and bought by Locker Trawlers in the 1990s.
Under Skipper Dave Locker she works hopper trawls up to 350 miles from Whitby.

Cod landings showed a remarkable forty per cent increase during the first six months of 1998 compared with the same period in 1997.

The big codling fishery really took off in the Spring. Prices were good and it was a happy time when quality fish met a consistent demand.

Whitby has a reputation for excellent fresh fish which attracts a strong buying power.

The fishermen are known for taking a pride in their catches. Fish are well gutted and cleaned and iced in 7-stone boxes without being crushed by overfilling, and the keelboats have fishroom chilling equipment.

In 1994 the fishmarket was upgraded to meet European Union hygiene regulations and has two insulated and chilled auction halls, a fishbox washing and stowage area, and lavatories and wash hand basins.

It provides a pleasanter working atmosphere and enhances the appearance and saleability of the fish.

Some sixty per cent of inshore fish goes to local merchants for the superior British retail and restaurant trade.

Busy and bustling

At the start of 1998 a busy bustling fleet of static gear boats was actively involved in commercial fishing from Whitby including eight over 10m overall length and some twenty-three below.

Static gear is that which fishes passively and does not move such as gill and trammel nets, longlines, crab and lobster pots and salmon drift and beach nets.

The static gear boats included ten cobles, a handful of Whitby-built mini keelboats and a variety of fully decked vessels constructed elsewhere.

The coble, designed for beaching and sailing in a particular milieu, was giving way to non-localised types in wood and steel and GRP with wide transom sterns and greater deck area to carry and handle more fishing gear.

Some fishermen had sold or decommissioned their over-10m vessels and bought shorter ones to free themselves from the over-10m rule contstraints.

Perhaps the most singular addition to the under 10m fleet in the 1990s was the 32ft steel catamaran

STEELAWAY WY364 which Skipper Walter Walker built at his clifftop home at Port Mulgrave.

Her launch in 1995 down 300ft cliffs to the isolated and ramshackle silty harbour, once an ironstone exporting port, involved the use of pulleys and steel hawsers and earth-moving plant and enthusiastic volunteer helpers.

The static gear boats are flexible and resourceful and try different things at various times.

In 1998 for example a good number of them were starting to catch Dover soles on soft ground using shallow gill nets only 10½ 109mm meshes deep.

The big run of cod in the winter of 1997-98 was beneficial to the static gear fleet and one day the mini keelboat ROSE ANNE caught a mighty 260 stones of fish in her trammel nets.

Heebie jeebies

On occasion during the 1990s the potters have landed velvet crabs for export to Spain. Known as 'heebie jeebies' these are lively and give a nasty nip.

Whelk pots have been tried, but near Whitby these shellfish have thicker shells and a reduced meat yield and fetched lower prices than those fished heavily off the Humber.

Potting was excellent in 1997 with individual hauls reaching three hundred lobsters during the summer, after an early moult thought to result from mild weather earlier in the year.

But the summer salmon fishery is failing. Only half a dozen boats, mainly cobles, took part in 1997 and '98. Licences were more costly to renew and no new ones are available.

Catches were abysmal in 1998 with each boat catching only ten or so fish each day.

Dumping disliked

Whitby fishermen are determined to survive amid the many changing rules, restrictions and bureaucratic complexities by which the British fishing industry is surrounded in the late 1990s.

They are concerned about the dangers of overfishing but consider some EU and UK conservation policies unworkable and even counter-productive.

The quota system is disliked as it results in dumping dead fish at sea and the inducement to bypass the auction markets and sell over-quota catches illegally.

Quotas are a problem in mixed fisheries where many types of fish are caught. Eventually the allowable catch of one species is used up and dumping has to start.

Many fishermen would prefer technical conservation methods whereby fishing gear is adapted to retain one of several species captured and permit others to escape. Much research into selective gear has been carried out by European and British technologists and the fishing industry.

A Whitby firm, Caedmon Nets, worked closely with the Sea Fish Industry Authority and the National Federation of Fishermen's Organisations on the development of separator trawls which have two cod-ends, one above the other.

They were designed to catch flatfish and cod in the lower cod-end and higher-swimming haddock and whiting in the upper. Each cod-end had the appropriate mesh size to reduce the capture of immature fish from the different species.

Cod and flatfish require a much bigger mesh for effective escape of juveniles.

Many fishermen would like to see a policy whereby each EU coastal state would manage its own fisheries on a zonal basis geared to individual needs and circumstances, but with particular emphasis on technical conservation techniques.

Some would like to see the complicated quota system replaced by restrictions on the number of days the boats spend at sea but at a set rate for all and planned well in advance.

Others suggest the closure to fishing of certain areas of seabed including the cod spawning grounds.

Nets always need mending. This photograph was taken on the quayside in Whitby, probably in the early 1960s.

Nevertheless, Whitby has faith in the future.

Richard Brewer, skipper of ARRIVAIN 111, said "There is so much enthusiasm among the lads. Whenever suitable boats come up for sale Whitby men enquire about them".

Some of the keelboats alongside the fish quay in 1998.

POSTSCRIPT

The year 1997 was made extraordinary in Whitby by the two visits of HM Bark ENDEAVOUR, the superb Australian-built replica of Captain James Cook's eighteenth century vessel of exploration and scientific investigation.

ENDEAVOUR coming into Whitby on October 21st. 1997 for her second visit to her spiritual home.

Response to the replica was astonishing and awesome. Tens of thousands of people were enchanted by this rugged bluff bowed little three masted square-rigged sailing ship.

In May a colossal crowd numbering some 100,000 watched her sail into Whitby where the original ship was constructed as the coal carrying vessel EARL OF PEMBROKE in 1764.

Vast throngs of people queued for up to six hours to board the replica and explore her deck and interior.

ENDEAVOUR visited Whitby during a tour of British ports as part of her maiden world voyage. She returned in the autumn for a refit.

I helped to repaint her, and in January 1998 I had the life-enhancing experience of sailing aboard her from Hull to Plymouth before she departed for the USA.

Things maritime

It may appear odd to include her in a study of fishing vessels but it seems to me that nothing written about things maritime in Whitby in the late twentieth century can choose to ignore her.

Some mention must be made.

Maritime historians have said that the future study of traditional and historic vessels will move further towards the building and sailing of authentic replicas.

Commissioned in 1994 ENDEAVOUR is owned and operated in trust by the HM Bark ENDEAVOUR Foundation for the people of Australia, New Zealand and the United Kingdom.

Part of the Foundation's mission statement is to 'add to the understanding of the construction, performance and sailing techniques of eighteenth century vessels and HM Bark ENDEAVOUR in particular'.

The Admiralty in the eighteenth century liked to use Whitby-built colliers as dependable exploration ships. They were stalwart and full-bodied and had excellent handling, seakeeping and beaching qualities.

The replica has already proved herself to be an outstanding seaboat.

She measures 109ft 3in with 29ft 2 in extreme beam and draws about 14ft, and her mainmast is 127ft 11in tall.

ENDEAVOUR is classified USL 2A as a sailing cargo vessel with a working crew of professionals and experienced amateurs.

The main criterion in building her was to achieve historical integrity, though differences exist to satisfy modern safety requirements and enable her to maintain a tight sailing and visiting schedule.

Building materials including heavy durable Australian hardwoods were selected to give her a long life. Everything about her is weighty, massy and substantial.

Craftsmanship, standards of design and attention to detail are of the highest order.

The builders' philosophy was that nothing was too good for ENDEAVOUR.

Museum mode

ENDEAVOUR is 'ship' rigged, having square sails on all three masts. Though she sails when possible she has two Caterpillar 402hp diesel engines for use in unfavourable winds or when manoeuvring in restricted areas.

She looked very fitting in Whitby, the port which her captain, Chris Blake, referred to as being her spiritual home.

I was charmed by ENDEAVOUR and immensely curious about her. My short voyage with her was a magical experience. I have sailed aboard what is regarded as being one of the most beautiful ships plying the seas today.

GLOSSARY

Apron   Thick broad piece of timber abaft stem, to provide landings for the strake ends.

Bearding Areas in contact with the insides of planks.

Bevel   Edge of piece of timber, angled other than at rightangles.

Broach   Accidentally turn broadsides to sea and wind.

Bulkhead A vertical partition.

Buttocks   Rounded overhang of lower stern forward of rudder.

Cavitation   Collapse of air bubbles onto propeller blades, producing increased corrosion and spoiling propulsive efficiency.

Dead-fastened Passes through one piece of wood and part way through another.

Deadrise   Rise of bottom from keel to bilge.

Dipping lugsail   Quadrilateral sail on a yard hung one third the length of the yard from forward. Yard and sail are brought down and raised on other side of mast when the boat changes tack.

Displacement boat   Floats in the water rather than planing along the surface.

Drag   The keel is said to have drag when it is not level, but slopes towards the stern.

Entry   Fore part of hull below waterline.

Fair   Forms a continuous smooth curve without imperfections.

Fall   The hauling part of a halyard.

Flare   Outward curve of hull above waterline.

Floors   Structural members lying athwart keel (and athwart the hog in a coble) and continuous with the frames on either side.

Forefoot   Lower part of stem where it curves to join the keel.

Futtocks   Component pieces of floors and frames.

Gripe   Deep forefoot sets up resistance and causes boat to turn up into the wind.

Halyard   Rope for raising sail or yard up a mast.

Hard bilges   Round bilges with a tight turn.

Hollow lines   Concave areas of hull.

Hood ends   Ends of planks where they join into a rebate.

In way of   Adjacent to.

Inwire   Stringer running along inside the frames.

Jib sail   Foremost sail, set to bowsprit end.

Joggled   Notched to fit tightly across clinker planking.

Ketch   Fore and aft rig on two masts, with foresails, jib and mainsail on mainmast and mizzen sail on mizzen mast. Mizzen mast forward of rudder and mizzen sail more than fifty per cent area of mainsail.

Laid deck Deck made of narrow planks.

Lands   Overlaps of planks.

Leeway   Sideways movement.

Luff   Forward edge of sail.

Lugger   Boat with four-sided sails set fore and aft.

Mould   Pattern set up temporarily across keel as guide during planking-up.

Moulded   Either the measurement of a piece of timber between its curved surfaces, or the depth.

Offer up   Try a piece of timber in place to see if it fits.

Pintle   Vertical pin on forward edge of rudder.

Pitch   (of propeller). Distance boat would travel with one turn of propeller if there was no 'slip'.

Quarters   After ends of boat's sides.

Rebate   Recess cut in piece of timber to receive another.

Reef points   Short lengths of line used when folding part of a sail to reduce its area.

Rising stroke   Strake which starts the turn of bilge.

Rockered Curved fore and aft.

Roves   Small round copper washers.

Run   After end of a boat below water.

Sandstroke   (or garboard strake). Strake next to keel, or next to the hog in a coble.

Scantlings   Dimensions of pieces of timber.

Scarph   Joint used when uniting pieces of timber.

Seakindly   Behaves comfortably in heavy weather.

Seaworthy   Fit to go to sea safely.

Shaft logs   Chocks fitted inside and outside the planking to take sterntube through which propeller shaft passes.

Sheer   Curve of boat's top strake or gunwhale.

Sheerstrake   Uppermost strake.

Sheet   Rope attached to lower after corner of sail.

Sided   Either the measurement of pieces of timber between the straight surfaces, or the width.

Standing rigging   Fixed rigging which supports masts etc.

Stem   Forward end of centreline structure.

Strake   One complete length of planking from stem to stern.

To tack   Turn boat's head through the wind so that wind strikes the sails on other side.

Thwart   Transverse plank used as a seat.

Timbers   Transverse ribs when steam-bent to shape.

Traveller   Iron ring which travels up mast, and to which halyard is attached.

Tumblehome   Inward curve of boat's topsides.

Weatherly   Able to sail close to the wind without making undue leeway.

Yard   Spar set across a mast and normally supporting a sail.

SELECTED BIBLIOGRAPHY

Arranged alphabetically by name of author.

"The Wooden Ships of Whitby", Joseph Richard Bagshawe, Whitby 1933.

"Sail and Oar, A North Sea Sketchbook", Ernest Dade, 1933. Republished Ipswich 1988.

"The Chatham Directory of Inshore Craft", Consultant Editor Dr Basil Greenhill, Editor Julian Mannering, London 1997.

"Master Mariner Extraordinary", John Howard, Hull 1995.

"Spritsails And Lugsails", John Leather, London 1978.

"Inshore Craft Of Britain In the Days Of Sail And Oar", Volume 1, Edgar J March, Newton Abbot 1970.

"Sailing Drifters", Edgar J March, Re-issue Newton Abbot 1969.

"Fishing The Coastal Tradition", Michael W Marshall, London 1987.

"The English Coble", Editor J E G McKee, National Maritime Museum Monographs and Reports, No 30, London 1978.

"Working Boats of Britain", Eric McKee, London 1983, New edition London 1997.

"A History Of The Yorkshire Coast Fishing Industry 1780-1914", Robb Robinson, Hull 1987.

"Beach Boats of Britain", Robert Simper, Woodbridge 1984.

"North East Sail, Berwick To King's Lynn", Robert Simper, Newton Abbot 1975.

"Fishing Out of Whitby", John Tindale, Clapham, Lancaster 1987.

"They Labour Mightily", Dora M Walker, London 1947.

PERIODICALS

Classic Boat
Fishing News
Mariner's Mirror
Maritime Heritage
Model Shipwright
Motor Boat And Yachting
Wooden Boat
Whitby Gazette

REPORTS

Agriculture, Fisheries and Food, Ministry of; Sea Fisheries Statistical Tables (to 1993), Since 1993, UK Sea Fisheries Statistics.

North Eastern Sea Fisheries Committee; Fishery Officers' Reports.

Northumberland Sea Fisheries Committee; Fishery Officers' Reports

Sea Fish Industry Authority (formerly White Fish Authority); Annual Reports and Accounts.

SOCIETIES

The Coble and Keelboat Society.
The Society was founded in 1987 to bring together those interested in the traditional working boats of the north-east coast of England.
For further details, contact The Secretary, Edgar Readman, 20 The Green, Saltburn, Cleveland TS12 1NF.

40+ Fishing Boat Association.
The Association aims to promote the preservation of fishing boats and research into fishing boat heritage.
Contacts; Michael Crane, 63 Birch Hill Crescent, Onchan, Isle of Man 1M3 3DA.
Mike Smylie, Bron Menai Cottage, Dwyran, Anglesey LL61 6BJ.